fifty years of class
a teaching memoir

A. C. FISHER

ISBN: 1548786233
ISBN 13: 9781548786236

For Becky:

The newest teacher in our family

INTRODUCTION

"In the total expanse of human life there is not a single square inch of which the Christ, who alone is sovereign, does not declare, 'That is mine!'."

Abraham Kuyper

People were crying and hugging each other as if this was the end of their lives. I was doing none of this. Graduation from High School meant freedom. I couldn't wait to get out and tackle the world with a neat job in some cool office wearing great clothes. I had no plans for further education; I already knew it all. I was seventeen. The world awaited me.

I remember thinking that these girls I had seen walking to and from large office buildings in very high heels, chick suits with tight calf-length skirts, laughing with each other each morning must have been the happiest girls in the world. They were chic, making money and done with school. I wanted to be like them.

After graduation, I struck out one hot Paterson morning dressed to what was my conception of the nines, want ads and addresses in hand, to downtown offices for my first interviews. The men behind the desks (I think I did three that first day) each looked me over and said, "Come back in a few years." I knew they hired other high school grads, so what was this about? Did I really look that immature? I was not devastated yet.

When I got home that first evening, my mother said there had been a phone call for me from one of the deacons in our church. "What did he want?" I asked but she did not know, told me to call him back. I did. He offered me a scholarship to Calvin College for the coming school year. I was seventeen. I arrogantly declined the generous gift my church offered. Undaunted by that first day's experience, I made appointments for some more interviews later in that week. Again... too young. Too inexperienced. Too stupid to my way of thinking.

Happily, God is patient as were the deacons. After literally months of hoofing it all over Passaic County looking for that "dream" job; constantly being rejected because of lack of skills and a childlike appearance, in August, I ventured with trepidation to call the deacon back. "Yes", he said. "We've been saving it for you." I couldn't believe it but there it was. God does indeed move in mysterious ways. To top it off, Calvin accepted me at this eleventh hour with an application, most of which was conducted by phone.

In early September I was driven by my cousin and his wife, who had been visiting with us to Grand Rapids more than seven hundred miles from home to begin my academic career, which I had vowed never to pursue. The following four years became some of the best, fun-filled years of my life. I wept copiously when it was over.

I was not a good student. I spent more time having fun than studying. If someone offered to have a cup of coffee with me in the student center while I was on my way to class, more often than not I opted for the coffee and social time. Not something I recommend to my own students. However, I did manage to complete my studies, did actually learn a lot (thanks to a great faculty and rigorous demands) and managed to walk away with a BA in English Education, secondary level. My status ended up a little higher than in the middle of my class. I didn't deserve even that. I managed to get a few "A's" in Art (which I love) and in Dutch (which I could already speak).

Prior to graduation there was student teaching, which scared the heck out of me. I was afraid of having to teach in the one large, inner city school on Hall Street. When I received my assignment it was at the big inner city school on Hall Street. I girded up my loins (do women have loins?) as best I could. I met my supervising teacher with trepidation. He seemed OK and was encouraging. I walked into my first classroom with even more trepidation. It was a sophomore English class with a very diverse group of students. My next class was a sophomore honors class. Lilly white. I observed for a while and then was allowed to teach. But only the regular sophomores. As it turned out, I fell in love with the experience. What a total surprise that was.

At least one of the students was close to my age (twenty) and one was about six-four inches tall towering over me and looking like a growling bear. Some of these kids came from upper and middle class families. I can't recall how it all worked but it did. A very short, rather cute boy, I learned was stashing beer in his locker for lunch and had fathered at least four children by the time he was sixteen. Who would have guessed? Others came from very broken places deep in the inner city. A very big African American kid was a star athlete but no star when it came to academics. I was responsible for grading these students and could not for the life of me pass this young man. I did later check my student's files for other information and found his final grade had been altered to a "C". My first wake-up call.

Student teaching turned out to be a very enlightening experience. I managed to walk away with a poem dedicated to me written by one of the honors students and a full gift package of White Shoulders cologne and other products bought for me by the class. I also walked away with an abundance of relief that I had been given the grace to pull it off.

The next hurdle, of course, was to find a job. I interviewed at Muskegon Christian High with no success. One day I was called to the placements office at Calvin and found a principal from my past. He had been transferred from Eastern Christian, my alma mater in New Jersey to Kalamazoo Christian High in Kalamazoo, Michigan. He had asked for me, handed me a contract and said, "I think we already know each other so I would like you to work for me." Incredible! " I said Ok, signed the contract and that was that. My first year on my own was about to begin.

I had promised myself that I would stay in one place for only two years so after the second year at Kalamazoo Christian, I quit. Again, a rather selfish, arrogant move. I went home for the summer and began looking in school ads for a job. I sent my resume to Indiana. Agnes Kahler Middle School was in need of a sixth grade language arts teacher. I received a call to come for an interview, drove out there, did the short interview and was hired. My second job. Although I did enjoy the classroom and most of my colleagues, I knew that sixth grade was not my forte. So I didn't even give them a second year. I ran back to Kalamazoo and took graduate classes.

After attending Western Michigan University for two semesters following my time in Indiana, I ran out of money. My student loans were already astronomical so I quit that venture and took a trip to the Upper Peninsula of Michigan to visit with a friend. I was broke. Becky (the friend) told me about a new friend of hers who had just gotten a job at Gladstone High School, but it was a very difficult place to get into. I should try Escanaba instead. Apparently Gladstone was a more desirable place to teach so "everybody" wanted to work there. I thought I'd give it a try anyway so gave them a call. The principal hired me over the phone! Apparently the then Senior English teacher wanted to be a full time guidance counselor and my calling at just the right time gave him the opportunity to do that. Becky and her new friend were astounded, as was I. I worked there for nine years.

When I finally decided to move back to New Jersey, I applied to be a substitute teacher. I worked at both Midland Park High School and Eastern Christian. A full-time position opened at Eastern Christian. I was hired. Following twenty-eight years there, teaching both English and Art, I took early retirement and moved back to Michigan. Not enjoying days of leisure, I applied for a long-term substitute teaching job at Western Michigan Christian High in Muskegon. Again, without hesitation, they hired me. When the time came for the full-time teacher to return the principal struck a deal with her which allowed her to stay home to be a Mom and me to continue on teaching Senior English and AP. I was offered a contract to teach those classes the following year. It was to be part-time. Perfect! I taught both English and Art for five years before returning to New Jersey where I now teach at the local community college.

That about sums up the fifty years and it seems with the Lord's will there may be a few more. The point of all this rather mundane listing of my jobs is that I am not in control of my own life. God continually opened doors for me and equipped me to do the work. I had my failures in the classroom to be sure, but for the most part it has been a blessed fifty years and I can only pray for forgiveness for all the times I did not do my very best for all my students.

1

CLASSROOM AMBIENCE

Smell is a great reminder of past experiences. I remember the smell of my second grade classroom in grammar school in Winter. Chalk, radiator heat, wet clothes hung on hooks to dry, books and paper as well as lead (graphite) mixed together to identify a classroom. I loved that smell. It was in Paterson New Jersey, just down the steep hill from Prospect Park. The old brick building has since been torn down but my memories are stuck in the fibers of my body, especially the senses. I loved the cozy safety of a warm room, booming and banging out its heat from the ancient radiators and the sight of the snow-covered roofs of Sixth Reformed Church, the corner grocery and nearby houses just outside our windows on the third floor. The smell of that room as I entered always promised a good day. I loved the classroom then and I still do. But things have changed over those many years. Smells have changed and virtually disappeared.

The modern classroom has no good smell of its own. There is a white board, perhaps but no chalk. The odor of the markers for that board is caustic at best. The computers, cell phones, even the desks are free of any smell suggesting safety or warmth. Plastic does not convey cozy like wood does. There are books and papers and pencils which may offer a hint of something good, but one needs to put a nose right on or in to achieve that experience. Is there still paste, the kind some of us used to eat? It too had its wonderful odor. What was it like? Metallic peppermint maybe. At any rate, most of the familiar classroom smells of the past are virtually gone. What are our children going to have to bring them back to those rooms?

I taught high school for most of my fifty years in the classroom as a teacher. The pleasant odors of my own childhood did not exist there either, but the smell of paper, books, chalk and wood were often still present. When I began teaching College classes, alas, no odors, no smells except clothes and bodies. Nothing to make me feel any of the joy of being in a classroom. I still enjoy the classroom but not because of olifactory experiences.

2

MIDDLE SCHOOL ISSUES

When I was in fifth grade (I think), I was sent to the principal for something. I can't remember what, talking too much probably. He questioned me about my behavior, pulled out his ruler and whacked me on the hand a number of times. He checked my face for tears but there were none. I refused to cry and give him any kind of satisfaction. I hated that man. I also hate corporal punishment, especially by anyone not one's parents. I could tolerate a whack from my father at times, maybe.

It was a Middle School in Dyer, Indiana and I was assigned to teach Language Arts to sixth graders. Not really something I had ever considered. However, I agreed to do it for a year. The school was using an old building that had been the high school perhaps in the previous century. It was of ancient brick just across the parking lot from the newer contemporary structure. All the sixth grade classes were taught there. I was on the second floor.

In Winter my colleagues and I had to cross a very cold, icy parking area to reach our building from the main building. But once inside I delighted in my ancient room. The radiators were still there hissing their welcome to us in the cold winter months. I loved the smell of that room in early mornings on chilly days. There is an aroma emitted by radiator heat that is a bit metallic, a bit dusty, and a whole lot comforting. There is nothing like the embrace of pipe-knocking, water-pumping radiator warmth accompanied by the musty perfume of chalk dust, leaden smell of graphite, and oily smell of much walked over old oak floors. Any seasoned teacher would have to concede to the truth of this.

As much as I loved that old building and all the memories it elicited, I was not fond of teaching sixth graders. The maturity level of sixth graders is very disparate. The girls are a bit more mature and already interested in boys; the boys for the most part are interested in playing sports or other games. When I had playground duty (a real negative assignment) many of the girls would literally hang on me and ask for advice or tell me about their crushes and problems. I don't mind listening or even offering advice but I cringe from a group of little girls hanging on me. The boys ignored me and the girls entirely. Except for one boy.

David was thirteen going on eighteen. He lived at the local orphanage for boys. He had had some social and behavioral problems in his recent past which had resulted in failing grades as well as discipline procedures. He had been left back as well. That was a norm in the sixties for non-academically inclined students. It did not do David nor his immature classmates any good.

Within that warm otherwise trusting environment of my classroom there lurked an odious truth which required my attention. I hadn't noticed it until we had begun doing some group work. David LOVED group work because he got to sidle up very close to any number of girls. His eyes betrayed his motives and I watched closely to ascertain the extent of his enjoyment of feminine classmates, all of whom were still too immature to understand David's attempt at proximity.

When I pulled him aside to discuss this behavior, I had to make sure he had no clue as to one of my underlying reasons for separating him from group work.

"David." I said. "You are obviously more capable than the classwork on the sixth grade level. (I wasn't making this up, by the way.) I perceive an ability in you that we need to address. What do you think? Want to try something else?"

He grinned his charming little grin even at me. Exceptionally white teeth gleamed, dark Spanish-Indian eyes sparkled, thick lustrous locks of black hair moved to and fro as David heartily nodded his assent. He was a short boy but more than ready to be in a higher grade than sixth. So I put him on the individual SRA reading lab that we all had in our rooms at the time. These are individualized reading labs which allow students to perform reading and response activities at their own speed and assess themselves for each level. David literally zoomed through the labs until he had finished the entire set in about two weeks. No more group work in sixth grade for this boy.

I took his results to the principal, spoke with him about David's need to be with students his own age and together we decided to place David in the seventh grade although it was not yet even mid-term. Of course, David was consulted as well as his guardians but there were no dissenters and he was removed from my care to the care of the seventh grade Language Arts teacher. Was this a success? Yes. On all levels. He came to me with his grades at the end of the semester and beamed his happiness at having earned B's.

The other young man I had to watch in that class was a whole different kind of lad, rather more immature than his peers.. Ricky was a very small boy with a very impish little face topped by a blond crew cut which sported a cowlick just above his left eye. On the first day I sat behind my desk (before the students arrived) and opened all the drawers just to see what to expect in terms of space when I discovered a paddle in the bottom drawer. My colleague across the hall informed me it was to be used on any student I deemed a problem. When my students arrived I informed them that I had a paddle but would not use it. I did not believe in paddling. Ricky beamed.

He challenged me every day.

"Ricky, sit down."

"No."

"What? I said sit DOWN."

He did.

"Ricky, stop talking."

"Ricky, put that chalk down."

"Ricky, keep your eyes off other peoples' papers." He tested me every day. I did not want to resort to what he was challenging me to do but there is a limit to my endurance. I finally pulled out my paddle. The class gasped and then smiled. They were also tired of Ricky.

"OK. Apparently this is what you want. Out in the hall, Ricky." I summoned my colleague from across the hall to be the necessary witness, told Ricky to bend over and I let him have it. One really good one. When I slammed that paddle into his behind it gave me no pleasure. But I believe it had given him some.

He never misbehaved again. He didn't need to. He had won!

I am appalled now, when I reread this that I actually fell for this kind of discipline. It should never come to anything physical in a school. Parents might swat a behind from time to time as a reminder for proper behavior but others should never resort to the same.

When I got to Gladstone High a number of years later I was once again confronted with "The Paddle". It was still legal to use in some states. I overheard many conversations in the teacher's lounge about various forms of discipline used by my colleagues, but the most appalling were from a few of the coaches who delighted in retelling their stories of paddling boys so hard they were literally lifted off the ground. This kind of brutish behavior should not have been tolerated but it was. It reminds me of the same sort of thing in "Dead Poet's Society" where a boy can hardly walk after having experienced the paddle. Shame on us for having allowed this for too long. However; now we can't even put an arm of comfort around a grieving student for fear of being called out as a predator of some kind. Oh, how the pendulum swings!

3

WITNESSING DIFFICULTIES

Craig was one of my sixth graders at Kahler Middle School in Dyer, Indiana.. A bright and cute kid with freckles and a blonde crewcut; he smiled a lot. He was easy too have around.

We went to the library to do some researching and reading. We were doing a little "I Search" project. I sat at a table ready to answer questions and offer whatever help was needed. Craig walked over and sat opposite. He didn't really say anything for a while and I waited. He screwed up his face into a question mark and began to articulate a rather interesting question.

" If God exists, and He is supposed be loving, why do we need help or saving, like the church says. ("Initiating discussion about any specific religion as one's own faith [especially Christian in the 21st C.] is so not Politically Correct that one could get fired from teaching for doing so.) However, Craig asked the question. I don't even know why he thought I would be able to answer. But he apparently expected it.

"Well. I guess it might be something like this. Suppose you found a way to make tiny things that resembled you in a lot of ways and you magically made them come alive. You would really love them, right?

"Yeah, I guess."

"After all they are yours and you made them. However, one day they decide they don't want anything to do with you and they sort of spit in your face. What would you do?"

"I guess I'd just smash them and maybe start over."

"Yeah, that's what we would do. But God loved us, who are these tiny creatures he made to be like him 'in his image'. Our first father and mother turned to God and sort of "spit" in His face, wanting to do things completely on their own. Instead of obliterating us, His creation, He decided to save us by taking the "smashing" we deserved on himself in the form of Jesus."

Craig just looked at me and said little. "Ok, I guess." And went back to work.

It's hard stuff. But sometimes we are simply asked to give an answer the best we can. And sometimes our best just isn't good enough.

An interesting aside of this is that many years later I was home watching the TV gameshow, "The Price is Right" and there was Craig bidding on some stuff, a contestant.

4

WITNESSING GONE AWRY

I find so-called "witnessing" very difficult. I prefer to give an answer when asked. I think that's a Biblical stance. Anyway one particular situation my colleague and I encountered leaves room for nothing but hilarity. Mark, my colleague; Kathy, his wife, my husband and I found a way to take students on ten-day trips to Europe, Turkey and Africa while teaching at Eastern Christian High in North Haledon New Jersey.. We did this together for thirteen years.

We often had thirty or more students on our trips. We needed this many to fill a tour bus so that we did not need to share with another school. The situation we encountered on one of our many trips lends itself to more than just a smile. We had fewer students than we needed to fill a tour bus so the tour company added a very small group of students from Delaware to share the trip through Italy with us. There were many negative incidents due to this unwelcome alliance, to be saved for another chapter. But the best occurred one night in Rome.

As preparation we make it very clear to our students that they are not allowed to drink anything alcoholic on any of these trips regardless of the rules in any particular country. They also have to follow strict rules about curfews and fraternizing with students other than those in our own group.

At about ten in the evening, in a nice little hotel, more like a pensione than a hotel in the middle of Rome, four Delaware boys left the building, walked down the street to a small store and came strolling back with about four bottles of wine each. This is all very legal in Italy. Their chaperone had conveniently gone to her room at eight pm letting the young men fend for themselves, which they did with aplomb. Their room, unfortunately was just across the hall from a few of our girls.

At about 11 pm one of my colleagues and I did our rounds. We heard a little commotion down one corridor, made our way down there and found two of the boys knocking on the door of our girls. The girls, giggled, opened the door and were about to allow entrance by the wine bearing young men when I interposed. I sent the boys back to their own room telling them in no uncertain terms they are not welcome to engage in any way with the girls etc... then I went into the girls' room. I was angry. They'd been warned.

"Never. Never let these guys into your room. Don't open the door when thy knock and don't talk to them after curfew in your room. In fact, don't talk to them at all!" I said rather emphatically.

One young lady, sitting on her bed, in all the innocence she could muster, looked me in the eye and said, " But, Mrs. Fisher. How can we witness to them if we can't talk to them?"

You think I'm stupid, I'm thinking? Are you serious?, I am thinking. But I simply reply' "God does not expect you to 'witness' after curfew, to boys you don't know, carrying wine for some ungodly purpose. Trust me on this!" I was livid. How dare she. I closed the door and we continued "chaperoning". Needless to say, we got almost zero sleep that night.

Kathy, my colleague's wife heard more noise, girl noise that is, coming from the Delaware boys room. One of our girls was apparently already in the boys' room and in process of removing her shirt when Kathy walked in. What kind of witnessing was this kid doing?. Kathy couldn't believe her eyes. "OUT!" she shouted. We should have sent some of these kids home on the spot but the shirt remover was not going to a very disciplined home, we knew, so we kept her with us. We got little sleep on that trip.

These same Delaware boys for some reason found it great fun to frame our kids for doing all kinds of really offensive and damaging stunts. One morning in a very small very quaint hotel in an equally quaint village north of Rome, we were ready to leave our hotel when the owner came running out to the bus demanding to speak with Mark and me. It appeared that the shower head in one of our boy's rooms had been placed on the floor with the door open and turned on full blast. Water was everywhere. As it turned out our boys denied any involvement but they had left their door unlocked when going down for breakfast. That was a mistake since it gave Delaware access to the room. Mark cleared up the problem with the owner. When we got on the way the major offender of that group innocently chimed, "Was there a problem with water back there?" If I had had a whip....or worse.

The next day we stopped overnight in a really tiny hotel way out in the Italian countryside. There was one master key which was left on the inside of the great front door so it could be locked at eleven pm and opened for an emergency.

We were again on the bus when the owner ran out demanding to talk to Mark and me. "My key is missing!" he exclaimed. "It will cost more than four hundred dollars to replace it and change all the locks. Who has my key?" Mr. most obnoxious Delaware heard this and announced, "If we all anteed up some money he could repair the problem. Wouldn't that be a good idea?" Wise, wise Mark very calmly approached the students. He told everyone to get off the bus, our group was to take one side of the hotel and Delaware was to take the other. Each group would very slowly comb the interior of the building until the key was found. Soon one of our boys found the key lying on the stair recently used by the Delaware group.

These young men were not simply mischievous. They were delinquents at best. At the end of the trip their teacher proudly showed us a four hundred dollar gift her favorite boy who had already earned the nickname, sleeze bag (the worst one on the trip) had bought for her. She was either extremely naive or just willing to shut her eyes to the truth and gain the rewards.

She was not bad herself but she allowed evil inclinations from her kids. Most of her students were not really "bad" in and of themselves either. But, one, the ringleader was. His devious mind led the others to do what they might otherwise not have done. Who knows?

Evil comes in all kinds of forms and most often is the result of wrong thinking.

Teaching that truth comes so beautifully in much of great literature And sometimes through teachers.

5

CHRISTIAN PERSPECTIVE ON CLASSICS

Les Miserable is a daunting novel especially for high school sophomores. But I assigned it every year anyway. Daunting is good. My Sophomore Honors Humanities class was assigned a pretty long reading list for the summer and *Les Miserables* was the longest novel on the list Groans were ignored but I did eliminate the ponderous chapters Hugo included about his view of both politics, Napoleon and the church.

One of my favorite little lines is "Napoleon, the butcher of Europe." I read that and a few other ripe and juicy lines aloud to the class just to let them get a taste of the wit and very strong views of Hugo who could apparently not resist including all kinds of sermons and opinions in his works. He makes it all fit but an abridged version of the text, with simply the main characters and plot line is enough for less developed or interested readers to get the gist and power of the work. After all, that is what the play is about. In writing classes I tell students that less is best. "Do not use two words where one will do." according to Jefferson. I'm afraid Hugo used four words too many where only would have done the trick; even so what great work!

I tell my students often that "there is nothing new under the sun", only the tools change. Humanity at its best and at its worst is and has been and will be, I'm sure 'til the end. So a character like Jean Valjean, who represents and exercises mercy beyond comprehension after having received the same from God via a humble Bishop is someone we can love just as Javert, who knows and represents only justice without mercy is someone we can hate. But he too requires compassion from the readers. He needs to support the "LAW". He is not wrong, just too... However, as we discuss these characters I want students to see that neither man is totally good nor totally evil. Hugo does a rather neat job of offering backgrounds that give psychological and spiritual depths to the behavior of both characters. We end up sympathizing with Javert's suicide as much as we mourn for Valjean's death.

At the end of their senior year the honors students in Humanities at Eastern Christian had to present their life views in a project including those works which had influenced them the most. Most of the students included **Les Miserable.**

I mention this because there is such a powerful witness in this book about the love of God and redemption. I couldn't come close if I used my own words, in fact, I'd probably turn most of the kids away.

Some of the other redemptive novels we read are, **Crime and Punishment** by Dostoevsky which shows the redemptive power of guilt and confession. The strongest line in that novel comes from the poor little prostitute, Sonya when Raskalnikov, the murderer yells at her,"What has God ever done for you?' and she answers quietly and simply, "Everything."

He is saved through her love and commitment which brings him to humble confession. However, one of my students raised her hand after we discussed this phenomenon and said, "But he's a murderer, how can he be saved?" Aha..a question requiring me to delve into "witnessing". "Christ's sacrifice saves even murderers." I say. She is incredulous and stubborn. "No. He's a murderer." She insists. So I have to remind her the only unforgivable sin is the sin against the Holy Spirit. This takes place in a Christian School, by the way and I know this girl knows the Bible. However, not well enough it seems.

Another really redemptive novel is by Graham Green, **The Power and the Glory** in which an alcoholic little priest is persued by a cruel

Communist regime in one of the Mexican states, Tobasco in the 1930s. The priest seems a coward and on the path to self-destruction but he cannot resist offering the sacraments to the poor of the poorest any more than he can resist alcohol. However, at the end he becomes a type of Christ in sacrificing his life for the sake of a murdering criminal and is able to confess his own guilt while alone is prison the night before he is shot. He becomes a martyr although he denies he can be named that because he so much fears pain and death.

Students don't gravitate to this book mainly because it takes the priest to so many different towns, other characters and situations that it is difficult for 15 year-olds to follow the sequence. However, once they "get it" the message is clear.

I use teaching of great literature for many reasons but also as a way to "witness". Milton, Donne, Herbert, Shakespeare and so many others all tell the stories of humanity as it is. Whether writing in 2016 or 1500. We are what we are. And we need help. Always have and always will.

6

BITS OF BULLYING

In the late sixties and early seventies I taught in Gladstone, Michigan. It was touted as one of the best schools in that area which is upper peninsula of Michigan. It snowed from October to May and it was a wonderland for me. But the atmosphere in the school was not always wonderful.

I was teaching high school senior English and art. Sports was a big deal. Football dominated the town and the school. The players were heroes. School colors were purple and yellow so the uniforms of the cheerleaders were mainly purple with accents of yellow. One of the girls on the squad was a bit overweight. As unfair as it seems now, the boys called her "Moby Grape". The young girl was highly offended but no one really called the boys on it. They may have been reprimanded but nothing more was done than that. Bullying was not named in those days.

I overheard students one day refer to my colleague in the English department as "Jungle Alice". She was a highly dignified and otherwise respected teacher. When I heard the same name applied to her a number of other times I had to ask. "Why do you guys (always the guys) refer to Mrs….as "Jungle Alice"? Her first name was correct. But "Jungle"?

I got an answer from one of the offenders. "Did you ever see her arms?" he said. No, I hadn't noticed her arms but the next time I saw her I made a point of looking at her arms. They were very hairy! Is this bullying? In the strictest sense, (PC style today) yes, it was, but I'm not sure she was aware of the epithet. My guess is she was but I always hoped not. Nothing was ever mentioned about that either. What would be the course of action today? Expulsion? I hope not. In fact I hope nothing except perhaps to let these boys know their immature behavior was hurtful to others.

As a teacher the only name I ever heard anyone refer to me as was "Sarge". And that only in one place and briefly. As far as I know. (I really didn't care.)

One other name I recall hearing over and over was applied to a girl in my class. All the boys(yes, all) called her "Manly". She did not appear overly distraught but I did catch her grimacing about it once or twice. Karen was tall and muscular. She had long blonde hair. I thought she was really cool looking. I asked again why was she called manly? but got no answer. Now here is how dense I can be. The student in question was probably gay and everyone but I suspected it. At some point I did figure it out but it took some time.

A much more serious situation occurred in the same school. It had nothing to do with bullying. I only learned of it from the students, many who had no qualms about sharing the information. A very pert and pretty senior in my class did housecleaning on a regular basis for one of my colleagues. He was single and had an apartment in town. This young lady spent more time at that apartment than necessary it seemed. When I heard that they were sleeping together I refused to believe it. He was in his mid-thirties and she was seventeen. Now it is a crime. He would be in jail and labled as a sex offender but then, it seems nobody thought too much of it. It seems, as I learned later, it was pretty common knowledge.

Another teacher showed movies almost every day. He was supposed to be teaching history, but the movies did it for him. When he showed me some of his film list I knew that many were graphically violent with little or no redeeming qualities. I wondered aloud if it was a good idea to show all this stuff almost three or four times a week. He grinned and said it made for easy lesson plans. The man was an ass and should not have been in the classroom.

It seems that the school in the UP was a den of iniquity and incompetence with no redeeming features, but that is not the case. I reveal some of its faults because these things were a part of my experience. The good stuff far outweighed the bad. I had many very dedicated students as well as colleagues. Even the name callers were not "bad". They were jokers and did not quite understand the harm they inflicted. I think.

One particular student responded to almost everything with "oh my god!" He said it without thinking at least twice per class period until I finally asked him, "Do you believe in God?"

"No." was his reply.

"Then why do you call on him so often?" I asked. He grinned and nodded., understanding exactly what I meant.

I loved teaching in that school. I loved living in the U.P.. I needed to leave after nine years there but have very fond memories of those students and colleagues. I especially miss my Art colleague. Anne was and is one of the most positive people I ever met. She laughed a lot, took students in who needed help, and helped me learn ceramics. She professed to be a Christian because she knew and said that she was "good". Belief in Christ as Savior? No. But good? Yes. And a ton of fun. I still miss her.

7

TEENS TALK /I LISTEN

The Art Room at Gladstone High was a hub bub of activity and noise. The ceramics people were either pounding out clay to remove air bubbles or pounding their feet on the manual wheel to create evenly thrown pots...or not so even as was most often the case. Conversation was not only allowed but encouraged. After all there were artists in the room. Artists need free expression.

Discussion revolved around life events as teens understood them. My students were discussing having children and birth and care of babies. Judell, a beautiful young student, was very animated in her response to a discussion on breast-feeding.. She offered a disgusted grimace when breastfeeding was brought up. "I'm never going to let some kid eat my body!" she yelled. The whole class quieted, stared, then snickered as she offered a deviant look over the room and went on with her project.

Discussions like this were not new to me. I took art when I was in Junior High (middle school now). My art teacher had seven children and loved to regale us with his home stories. He especially enjoyed talking about having children and what went into that process. I learned more sex education in that class then anywhere else including my home. Is Art an automatic catalyst for this? Maybe.

I once took a class to the Metropolitan Museum of Art in New York City. As we considered the art of the various periods, one girl came to me with a problem. "Why do we have to go to a museum to see all these naked people? I don't want to see them."

"Well," I answered. "Just don't look at them then." We continued on without further comment.

One of my colleagues who had accompanied us on this trip also had a "problem". "Why are there so many paintings of women with only one breast showing?" he wanted to know. I can't figure out if he thought this simply odd or if he would have preferred that both breasts be showing. I do think it was the latter but I didn't want to think about it. The answer to his question of course is "because *men* painted them".

Life drawing classes are very problematic for some people but very necessary for the proper drawing of anatomy. Even dressed figures require correct use of anatomy...unless stylized, elongated (like El Greco's figures) or completely abstracted (like many of Picasso's figures). And these classes also cause concern in many circles.

Anyway, art is very subjective although also very precise. Or something like that. Try to define it.

"Draw what you see" is one of the first things I like to teach. Draw a line at a time; do not try to draw the entire thing since you will be drawing a perception you have instead of it.. We begin drawing a small object and go to a still- life and proceed from there. Most students "get it". There are always some who don't.

When doing one and two-point perspective I had one boy who simply could not do it. Instead of a street in one point he would end up with straight horizontal lines going up to the sky and another slanted line crossing the first two through the middle. I showed him the dots (vanishing points) to follow but he inevitably ignored them in favor of some unrecognizable geometric figure having no relation whatsoever to the vanishing points. Poor boy...visually impaired? Some kind of impaired, I thought but I couldn't figure out what. At any rate, he did all right in other ways.

I'm just glad I didn't have to teach life drawing. High schoolers shouldn't have to deal with nude models. It's a fact that most, especially men don't deal with it very well either. Consider the life of Rodin or Picasso for verification of this. Models invariably became mistresses or worse.

8

PROBLEMS WITH STUDENTS

Teenagers are a unique group of people. One person once said,"I'd like to bury my son when he turns thirteen and dig him up again when he turns twenty." There is a reason for this sentiment.

A young man in my English class (n the U.P. again) just fidgeted and fidgeted in his seat. Or, he would suddenly get up and stand by his desk for a minute at a time. I told him on numerous occasions either to sit down or stop all the fidgeting, whichever it was. He didn't stop. After a short time of this I kept him after class. " You are disturbing the class when you stand or move around so much. What's the problem?" I asked.

He hemmed and hawed a bit. "It's a little embarrassing." He said.

"Well, try me anyway."

"Well, when I sit for any length of time my butt gets really sweaty."

"What?"

"Yeah and then it itches and I just can't sit anymore."

"So, What should we do about this? You can't drop out because of a sweaty butt, you know."

"Yeah. What if I lay down somewhere. I can take notes if I'm on my stomach."

I thought about this. I was very reluctant to allow such an absurdity but the sweaty butt boy needed a resolution. "Okay, we'll try. You lay down under the window, near the wall where you won't be obvious and we'll see how that works out."

He grinned and left. The next day found him lying there with notebook on the floor and pen in hand. In the middle of the class time there was a slight knock on the door. The English Department head (Jungle Alice) had noticed the boy on the floor and wondered what the problem was. "Oh, that. He has a sweaty butt and can't sit." I told her. She rolled her eyes and shuffled off down the hall without comment.

When dealing with a classroom filled with teens one must sometimes resort to very unconventional methods to accommodate very specific issues. One does one's best. One must be creative and have a sense of humor.

But things are not always easy or funny. Students sometimes disappear. It was the Vietnam Era, after all, and one of our most troublesome students went off to war. We were glad to be rid of him. Before that school year was over, he was a casualty. No amount of misbehavior in high school is worth that. Years later I found his name on the Vietnam Memorial in Washington DC. One does not want to be rid of a student in that way.

One year I had a study hall assignment filled with almost a hundred students. Awful. One day a seat was empty. "Where is Brian?" I asked a student. Silence. Then, "I thought everyone knew" one girl ventured. "He went fishing with his father this past weekend and got caught on an overhanging branch that pulled him out of his boat and submerged him. He drowned." I almost fell off my chair. No one had told me.

These kinds of stories were not new to the U.P. One of my students and his friends went to the local dump looking for "stuff," also for bears which were known to frequent the area. The boys found an empty Pam container and thought it would be fun to get high on the remaining gas. "Jason" was the first to inhale. He died on the spot. He was an only child. What would his parents do now?

Another, whom we thought mature and wise, went off one holiday weekend to a friend's "camp" (Everyone it seemed had a hunting cabin in the woods referred to as "camps"). They had a few beers, a lot of laughs while shooting off fire crackers. One went off in Daryl's hand. He lost the hand. What did I say about teens?

They love fun, can be exceedingly stupid while having it and cause them- selves and others irreparable harm. Car accidents while speeding on dark country roads also took a few of our students. These were the difficult times. Saying a final "goodbye" to kids. The irony is that too many parents do bury their teens but they don't get the chance to dig them up again.

9

LOSING THEM

Bears have hairy arms but they don't live in jungles. They have now been sighted in most of the States but they have always been pretty prevalent in the Upper Peninsula. My students and colleagues talked of eating bear meat. Venison I like. I never had the opportunity to eat bear meat. My students often brought in smoked salmon they had caught and smoked but never bear.

One my fellow teachers was an avid hunter. It surprised me to learn he did not only eat bear but he hunted them with bow and arrow. He explained to me once that the bear came relatively close to him before he was sure he could get a good shot and shoot it so it had no chance of survival if all went wrong. Even if wounded, the bear would certainly come after him. So the sport was a risky one. The guy impressed me as nuts to take this kind of risk.

Hunters came up in large numbers from the lower peninsula during hunting season. November was cold but it brought them out in droves. The strange thing is that the local hunters went farther north or to Canada. The season lasted more than a week, as I recall and many students were absent during that time. School never closed, however.

It was also during this influx of hunters from below and the outflux of the locals that the bars were doing some of their best business. The problem was that the wives left behind found their time on their hands cumbersome and frequented the bars, met the new men and the rest need not be said. Sad stuff.

The drinking and subsequent alcohol related problems did a lot of damage. I found to my dismay there was something called the "Gladstone Divorce". Severely abused women used this to save themselves. It amounted to the drunken, violent husband coming home late at night or early morning ready to beat up his wife.

One incident in particular involved one of our school employees. She had had more than enough. One Saturday night she *knew* she had had enough. After her kids were safely in bed she took control. She waited behind the kitchen door with a knife in her hand. When her husband came stumbling in, cursing and calling for her, she stepped out and before he could hurt her she stabbed him right in the heart. He died and she was free. Finally. No charges were filed. It was simply referred to as "The Gladstone Divorce". In the end it was deemed as an "either it's him or me" self-defense situation.

I know I make the Upper Peninsula sound like a wild degenerate place. But let it be known we also had a wonderful Art Community, a number of very solid churches and Christian teachers on staff as well as others who truly cared about the students and were committed teachers. The rough incidents surprised me because I had been too sheltered, I think.

My own Christian School experience from grade one through college might not have prepared me for the world. Sin was in those schools and in my rather closed Christian community as well but murder and divorce in that time, the fifties, were seldom heard of. Probably kept under wraps. Or where there was real pain it was hidden behind closed doors and silent tongues.

The only real complaint about teaching in the public sector in Michigan at that time was the law that required me to belong to or at least contribute my dues to the teacher's union. I felt and still do that this is unconstitutional. I had no freedom of choice if I wanted to teach.(That law has since changed.) My biggest concern was what the Union both local and national stood for. One of the causes that my money supported was Planned

Parenthood, the right to choose abortion in particular. This went against my conscience but all public school teachers in many states had no choice but to support it.

Other than that I have fond memories of Gladstone High School, of the ice and snow which appeared in abundance but seldom closed us down and many of my very dear colleagues and students, all of whom are very old by now. I particularly remember one ride to school in heavy snow. My car fishtailed across the road right on the bridge over the Escanaba river. I was sure I was going in the drink, never to return. But I survived.

An interesting reason why the school wasn't ever closed due to snowfall was because the former superintendent always got in his car before six AM on stormy days and would drive up the Bluff (a hill resembling a very high dune). If he made it without incident, we had school. He always made it. The only times school was called was if the drifts were more than five feet high or the roads were totally covered with ice.

Even bear hunters had to stop then. But not much else closed us all down. People had skis, snowmobiles and a ton of hutzpah as well as heavy clothing. It is not Alaska, but close enough.

10

TRIPS AND HOME

The senior class in any school that I know takes some kind of class trip. In Gladstone, the senior class were bussed to St. Ignace on Lake Huron and taken on the ferry to Mackinac Island. The island lies east of the Mackinac Bridge which spans the straits of Mackinac. Lake Michigan and Lake Huron converge in these straits, often extremely turbulent and dangerous. No cars are ever permitted on the island. Travel is done by foot, horse power (literally) or bicycle. All the students know this. There are many varied shops as well as eateries. It is also the place of the famous Grand Hotel used in movies one of which is "Somewhere in Time". Its pool was used for a film starring Esther Williams. It is off limits to our students. Not because they were prohibited so much as there is a cost involved just to wander up to the front porch.

I was a chaperone on many of these trips. One in particular stands out. Apparently some students had gone there the afternoon prior to the day of the trip and stashed beer in the woods. This was news to me and my fellow chaperone, Ann who rode around the island with me on our rented bikes and helped me enjoy a delightful box lunch on the beach. We were told at least a week later by one of the senior girls. I only hope the guys had a roaring good time.

The only incident that might have alerted us to the situation was on the ferry on the way back from the island. We were close to port in St. Ignace when we heard commotion on the upper level. We went up there and heard shouting. There was a dare going on. "Go on, Jay, do it. We dare you." And "Hey, Jay, you can swim, go on, jump. We dare you." And "We'll give you twenty bucks if you jump! Do it." Ann and I ran to the rail yelling for them to stop just in time to see Jason take off into the murky, oily water on the side of the boat.

The stupid kid was a mess but did get back to shore safely and was hauled up. A member of the crew gave him a towel but he was soaked through, and I am happy to report, he shivered all the way back to Gladstone, a two-hour trip.

The boys responsible and Jason were disciplined by the administration, as well as by their parents. It's a happy thing when parents support the teachers and school in general when it comes to discipline. This doesn't happen so much these days and it is a real blight on education in general. No support from home means less respect for authority. How do you teach successfully with that?

I left the Upper Peninsula shortly after that trip, not because of the trip but because of the negative influence of a cult in my personal life.. My husband had aligned himself with a group of men who had made themselves subservient to an older man. This guy had been asked to leave a multitude of churches for his unorthodox leanings and behavior. Bill came home one day and told me he had "submitted" himself to this guy. I wasn't sure what that meant, exactly. As it turned out it meant that he was going to let this person rule his life and all OUR life decisions. For example, when I wanted to buy a new refrigerator, H… said we didn't need one yet so Bill refused to let us buy one. Bill never came home on time anymore because he was doing "the Lord's work" by chasing ambulances and telling the sick they did not need to be sick, that they would be healed through his prayer intervention. He also got fired from his job as a social worker because he would take his clients to H. for healing instead of to the various hospitals or safe-homes where he was assigned to bring them. He began lying about where he was, where he was going and many other things. Through the help and advice of a dear pastor friend I found the courage to leave. I felt that my husband had betrayed our vows by taking on a new and peculiar vow with this older guy. I was labeled "a rebellious woman". So I went back to New Jersey. It was a sad farewell to Gladstone High School. I had loved it there.

11

WHY I HATE SUBBING

I walked up to the long red brick building without enthusiasm. But I needed the job. When I got inside and entered the really old fashioned front office with its glass doors, ancient cubbyholes for mail and heavy wood counter top I was given the folder and told there were no lesson plans. "What?" I wanted to yell. The lady with the stringy yellow hair and bright red lips smiled patronizingly and said, "After all, he only had his accident two days ago and that was on the weekend. So how could he write lesson plans for the next two weeks?" I murmured an "oh". And looked inside the folder. Class attendance lists, rules and a handbook. I closed the folder. "These are English classes, right" I queried. At least I knew English.

"You can improvise, I assume?" she said. Yes, I would certainly do that.

Moving from the Upper Peninsula back to New Jersey was a bit of a culture shock. Especially because I didn't have a job. So, in desperation I did some substitute teaching. This was Midland Park High School. I subbed for three weeks. I hate substitute teaching.

On the first day in my first class I took role and had only one absentee to report. That was easy. I began by asking the students what they had studied, what was expected of them by the now defunct teacher with a broken ankle, what they would like to study next within the confines of the course. Stone faced silence met my questions. Later one student did venture to inform me about the course and we proceeded from there. At the end of that first class period a boy jumped out of the clothes closet in the back of the room. Just a bit surprised I asked who he was. He said he was the kid I probably had marked absent but, he was here after all. He had spent the entire class time hidden in the closet in the back of the room. He had come out with a grin. I told him I had indeed marked him absent. He replied that he was NOT absent but just a bit hidden. "Yeah, right," I replied. I handed in the absentee notice.

This was in Midland Park High School. I had taken a two-week assignment, covering for a very popular, lenient teacher who had broken his ankle. The time turned into three weeks. No lesson plans except the information that this was a class in English Literature. My specialty is English Literature. I made up my own lesson plans, assigned the reading of a book for the week, showed a film based on the book, wrote up a study guide and put the classes in groups to discuss the various questions together. I never allow students to answer questions without offering support/proof for their answers from the text. Of course there were many who never bothered to read the book and relied on others to provide the information. The others complained about doing all the work while some got away with nothing done. I told them the test would rectify the injustice. I gave an open note test requiring page and paragraph documentation for each answer. I graded as best I could but who knew what the grades actually meant when their own teacher returned? Not my problem, I did what I could.

One day a rather defiant young man in one of the classes took out a pack of cigarettes, Lucky Strikes, unfiltered; dropped it on his desk (he sat right in the front row) and dared me to do something about it. He didn't say so verbally, but his face, his expression did the job for him. He stared at me not blinking for what seemed like a whole minute. I stared back. No movement in the room, anticipation shouted silently as we assessed our situation, both of us determined and stoic. Finally, I stood in front of him and told him quietly to give me the pack. No, he wouldn't. Okay. Then I asked him to put them away. No, he wouldn't. Was I going to fight him? No, I wouldn't. I walked slowly to the classroom phone, called the office, told them to come and get this kid and went on with the lesson. There was an audible sigh from the class. I don't know if they were glad or sad that the confrontation was over without an actual fight. I hate subbing.

Some of the students were happy to have a teacher in the classroom to continue with English. This I learned from a student who bothered to tell me one day. It made me happy to continue. However, too many took advantage of the situation.

One student was in the class for a whole week before someone informed me he didn't belong there. He was skipping another class in order to be funny and sit in on mine. When I called role he just kind of disappeared under his desk, or something. At any rate there he was. I took him aside. Told him he was "caught", hoped he had learned something while there and I didn't want to see him again. I didn't. Maybe he had learned something in the few days he had spent in my classroom. And maybe not.

The administration might have had some inkling of all these shenanigans but I never found out what was done about them. I assume they were just glad to have someone in there willing to take the spot.

I had done some day- subbing in Kalamazoo many years before this. It was more like baby-sitting while students did busy-work but taking on a long-time assignment does give one the opportunity to actually teach, which is what it is all about, after all.

Subbing at Eastern Christian was a lot easier. However; babysitting was the only thing I really got to do. Bored students sat doing unimportant busy work, which I am convinced is rather anti-education instead of actual education. Not fun. I was possibly even more bored than the students. Any attempt at discussion was met with hooded eyes, silly grins and deadly silence. A very slight advantage might have been that both my oldest nephew and niece were both at E.C. at the time so I did get to see them in a different environment. I liked that but they didn't go out of their way to see me. I had turned a bit into the enemy, I think.

The following year Eastern Christian hired me full time. Subbing has its advantages. When I retired and moved to Grand Haven in Western

Michigan I was again asked to sub. Western Michigan Christian High needed a long-term sub and that would be the only kind I cared to do. The classes became "my own" so to speak. I was there for an entire semester and was hired to continue on for the next four years.

12

STUDENT MEMORIES

Writing is such an excruciating work as William F. Buckley once wrote that I have been sabotaged by writers block for the past three months. I became so frustrated by my inability to further this project that I actually succumbed to the temptation of using social media for help. On Facebook, I posted a request for students to come forward with any incidents or events they remembered from our class times together.

Give me good stuff and bad stuff I wrote, so there would be a balance in this memoir. No one is perfect and I knew there had to be those out there who had some very negative memories of me but I received none of those I did get a few interesting "anecdotes" and memories.

Matt wrote: "My senior year we were taking a quiz, not even sure what it was on (maybe Paradise Lost?), everyone was quietly waiting to begin working. You passed out the quizzes, then proceeded to look up a word or two in the dictionary. Next, you dragged the recycling bin over to the bookshelf and casually dumped the entire stack of reasonably new dictionaries (in very good condition) into the bin. Every student looked up in either sheer dismay, shock, or horror, but no one said anything - our faces said it all. After all of the dictionaries were in the bin, you saw our startled faces and said, completely straight-faced, "They didn't have a word in them. They are useless. Throw them out."

No one dared question you.

I am unashamed to say it is probably the most badass things I have ever witnessed from a teacher."

I do remember doing that and to this day am convinced that if something is not up to par in the classroom, throw it out. That includes teachers, by the way.

Becky also sent me a rather telling memory. She wrote: " Hi Mrs. Fisher!

I read your Facebook post and I'd love to send you a few memories that I have from class. I was in your 12th grade English class, and Art class at Western Michigan Christian. You have stuck out to me as a teacher in a way that I was not initially certain of. I was used to teachers immediately loving me because I raised my hand, answered questions, and had a lot of input in class.

However, at the beginning of your English class I felt like you got more annoyed with me. It took me a while to figure out why. When I took your Art class I got to see a different side of you and I finally understood why you wanted me to stop being so involved in English. You actually cared that we all learned. I think other teachers were happy to let me move the class along quicker with right answers (to the detriment of other students' work ethics). You didn't let me do that. I remember you teasing me a little in order for me to stop raising my hand while everyone else sat like spuds in their seats. At first, I thought you hated me. Then I realized that it was tough love. I also remember resubmitting papers left and right to get a better grade. It made me a much better writer. I felt like you challenged me more than any other teacher I have ever had, and for that reason I hold a very high respect for you. I also loved how you taught art. It wasn't about perfection but composition. You wanted something that was creative and real, not something that had no feeling or meaning. It was so refreshing.

I scrawled this out quickly, so forgive any grammatical errors. I saw your request and figured I could give you something to work with. Good luck!!! :)
--Becky"

Incredibly kind of Becky to interpret my behavior this way. Many students would not have been able to see it the way she does.

I'm not getting any slams, so sorry but this is Jordan's contribution.

"Mrs. Fisher,
     I saw your post on Facebook about writing your teaching memoir and thought of a memory I had from my senior year.
     It was the day we were reciting a poem in front of class and I had chosen a poem by William Wordsworth called 'The World is Too Much With Us'. I had rehearsed the poem countless times but when the time came to recite it, I froze. You encouraged me to get up on the desk and proceed with the poem and that gave me the confidence to relax and if my memory suits me accurately, the rest of the poem came to me. I believe this was right around the time we watched 'A Dead Poets Society' and you really helped bring that to life for me and for the rest of the class if I might momentarily speak for them. All flattery aside, you are my favorite teacher to this day and I hope I can inspire others in the way that you did for me.
Jordan"

The best part of this entry by Jordan is that he hopes to inspire students or others (in whatever work he is doing). Who can ask for anything better than that from a student?

     It is also an eye-opener when a parent or two share a story from years ago when their child came home with this:

We were studying *The Odyssey*. I was showing "O Brother, Where Art Thou". This is the story Lydia brought home to her parents. "Mrs. Fisher told us there would be some bad words in the movie. She said most of us were familiar with these words so just deal with it or if you can't go stand in the corner, face the wall and suck your thumb." Her mother told me yesterday that in a Christian school there often is cover-up for sin when actually we need to be aware of the real world, filled with stuff like in the movie. She said when Lydia told her this she knew she would like me. However, I do not remember the incident so well but I am sure I did not say "suck your thumb", I did probably say "If you don't like it just suck it up".

> Hi Mrs. Fisher, I'm back in Michigan visiting family and friends this summer, and I stumbled across the song I composed to memorize "The Love Song of J. Alfred Prufrock." I remember you asked for a copy of it. I wanted to also let you know that "high school teachers" recently came up in conversation with some friends from WMC. I distinctly remember AP English with you - going to your house and that coffee shop off of Seaway Dr. - I made some pretty great memories in your class and learned how important it is to be honest and devoted to my work. Thanks for everything! - Bethany

One never knows, really what affects those with whom one comes in contact, whether as a teacher, parent, colleague or any other relationship. The best advice then is to be careful of what you say and do… always. This is one of my greatest challenges since I am excessively prone to sarcasm which is not always good in the classroom.

13

CHEATING

Joey. He was brilliant, I think. He was in Honors classes, had the highest GPA in his senior year and was in my English class. Honors. AP. The works.

I gave vocabulary lists once a week and a quiz at the end of each week. (This is more necessary today than ever due to tech usage, texting lol.) One day two students stopped by after class and informed me that Joey had been consistently cheating on his vocabulary quizzes. I hated and still hate this kind of information. However, I was grateful for the heads up. It is so difficult to catch someone at it and I told the students that I would need to keep a sharp eye on Joey and catch him at it myself.

When it came to exam time I offered (as I often do) an alternative assignment to the regular kind of exam (Multiple Choice, Essays etc.). I love to offer a challenge and see who is willing to take me up on it. I also believe it is tremendously beneficial to introduce new material in a different format at exam time. It keeps students on their toes and far from the cramming of material at the end. Cramming is not learning. So I prefer to try an alternate route for those who really feel up to a new challenge.

T.S. Eliot is one of my favorite poets. I offered the class to memorize "The Love Song of J. Alfred Prufrock" in lieu of taking the exam. We had studied it so it was not difficult new material although it is difficult, in some ways. More than half the class signed up to do this. They had about three weeks to prepare. Each student had the choice of reciting it to the class or me privately, or to write it out during the regular exam time. Joey was up for the challenge.

He opted to come to the exam and write his out. Fine. He sat apart from his classmates who were writing furiously and did his own furious writing. As I watched him I noticed he was looking down at his crotch area every few minutes. I quietly walked over to him and asked him to stand up. As he did a small slip of paper appeared from under his thigh. I picked it up. It was the entire poem written out in tiny print. "Joey, what's this about; why are you cheating?" I asked.

"I wasn't; that must have fallen out of my pocket when I sat down." He replied. It was paper and too small to just fall out of a tight jeans pocket. So when I mentioned that impossibility he changed his story and said, "Someone else must have left it there before I came in." No, No one else had sat there nor had anyone else opted to write the poem out during the exam time. I took his paper, took the tiny note and sent him to the principal to explain what he had done. After class I went to the office where Joey sat with Doug, our principal. I explained the situation. I showed Doug the "cheat note". Joey held to the story that it might have fallen from his pocket but we all knew this was absurd. I said he would fail the course for cheating and lying and left it at that. Doug agreed that it would be ok. A few days later Joey's father showed up. He supported his son and told me Joey knew the poem forwards and backwards. I said I believed that but he still had a cheat note and was using it so I had no recourse but to submit the failing grade. Father Joe was a big shot business man and frequent contributor to the school. I found out later that Joey would still be the valedictorian. I went bonkers. "How does this make sense?" I loudly queried of Doug. He simply said it was a done deal.

To this day I regret not having walked out of the graduation ceremony when Joey got up to speak. As it was, his peers simply snickered when he walked to the podium and did not pay him heed. I hope his father is proud.

Apparently cheating is so profound an epidemic in education and business (who knows what else) that one cannot know whom to trust. When I was teaching at Atlantic Cape Community College we were told to begin with a unit on cheating. The surveys in my classes indicated that at least eighty percent of the students had cheated on exams and tests one time or another. So I suggested that perhaps if you cheated your way through school you would end up with a high GPA but you were still *Stupid*! Having learned nothing. They almost all agreed. One young lady actually claimed she learned material from having cheated. Lying to oneself is even more insidious. As well as negative character development.

14

INTERESTING CHEATING

There are many ways to cheat. Lying, stealing, reneging on promises, are just a few. The bane of my life has always been grading papers. Cheating on a paper is easier with the internet than it has ever been. So my bane grows more severe.

I allow students to rewrite papers as many times as needed. They receive the grade on their final one. There are always deadlines, of course but some students have been known to rewrite at least eight times. Not fun for either of us but it is a golden way to learn to write and edit.

We spend numerous class hours on the problem of Plagiarism. I alert my students to the fact it is so easy to do but that if I find it the consequences are automatic failure of the course. Warnings upon warnings and even then someone will blatantly do it. Do they think I'm stupid? Do they hope I really don't comb through these papers? Think again. I hate it but do it.

In my literature course at Atlantic Cape Community College a paper appeared with undocumented little known information about Jane Austin. We had discussed plagiarism to a fault. The college handbook is very specific about what it is and the consequences. I marked the paper and told the student he may rewrite and document the offending passages.

Plagiarism is the issue but he got the opportunity to correct his error instead of failing outright. It came back without documentation and a totally bogus Works Cited page. The Semester was over. The paper went into my file. I emailed a letter to the writer explaining the issue. I got no response. I took the paper and a copy of the email letter to the Dean of Humanities as well as to the head of the department. Both agreed it was plagiarism and supported my decision. All was well.

One full year later I am suddenly required to meet with the student since he now has appealed his failing grade. A full year later. I am livid. I refuse to meet with him. I am called unprofessional by the new dean. I explain what happened and that I was supported. It is over. Guess again. Finally, after much harassment by this new dean I cave in and agree to meet this kid in the company of one of the counselors. I have the offending paper with me as well as the internet sites he "stole" and the cover letter I had sent him. (thankfully I kept the entire file.) I show the lot to the counselor and the student. The young man bows his head, says "I'm sorry, I need to retake the class and it will cost 400 dollars because my assistance won't pay to retake a failed class." I tell him I wish I could help. He cheated, he paid the consequences. The counselor agreed. The integrity of the college was also at stake. This is hard stuff.

One other, even more interesting incident took place at Eastern Christian. Melissa was in Humanities, an honors English class, team taught. She handed in a paper including parts I knew no high school student could have written. She was alerted of her error but insisted all the information was completely her own. I found the offending passages in another source. Her mother decided to come to school to support her daughter. We met. I showed her both the paper and the passages from the original source. They were of course, identical. My colleague and I explained the problem and the seriousness of plagiarizing. Her mother defended her. She said, "Melissa has a photographic memory so whatever she reads stays in her brain. She read these pages and put the information down as her own because it was in her brain. So it really is her own, you see." Neither I nor my colleague saw. We shook our heads in disbelief. "Whether she read it and memorized it or whatever, it is still another's information and requires documentation." We told them. End of story. No happy mother, no happy child. The argument was simply too absurd.

It is difficult especially when a parent gets this kind of defensive. It would be easy to back down but then where would we be?

15

DECEPTION

Deception is even more insidious when perpetrated by the educational system. I began teaching at Atlantic Cape Community College assigned to teach classes in remedial English for students who did not pass the entrance English exam. (ACCC has an open door policy but tests and requires students to pass the initial tests before sending into the credited programs.) There are two levels students must pass to get into the regular English program, Eng.007 and Eng.008. I taught both. Quite an eye opener.

There were some students who could not compose even one correct sentence let alone a coherent paragraph. We struggled through exercises, grammar rules, handbook chapters, short paragraph assignments and anything else I could think of. There were students who literally flew through these classes and continued on with much success. But there were too many who did not. I inquired about the various high schools these people attended. None of the incompetence made sense to me. Until one day the adjunct who used my room just after me came in early enough for a little chat. She was the librarian at one of the local high schools so I asked her what the problem might be in terms of the students' lack of English writing ability. "Simple," she said. "In Atlantic County no one is allowed to fail. We have to pass everyone regardless of achievements."

I was appalled. I and others got to teach students what they should have learned in grade school.

No accountability for the students would cipher down to no accountability for teachers as well, would be my guess. I know there are many tremendously dedicated teachers but there are far too many who love good pensions, summers off and 8-3 work loads. Any good teacher knows; however, that real work loads are from 8am-10 pm and Summers are spent on tamping up one's own education.

Anyway, Christina approached me after class on the first day of level 007. She informed me she has an IQ of 62 because of birth issues. She wants to get her associates degree in order to teach or aide young children. Will I help her with her writing? We'll see how it goes, I tell her and help in whatever way possible. Sorry to say the young woman could not put a sentence together. The frustration level was pretty significant.

After many weeks and many rewrites I decided to have a small talk. I simply explained that perhaps academics was not her gift and she ought to find what her gifts really are and pursue education in that direction. That evening I received a scathing, well- written email, signed by Christina that I was very unprofessional and ought to be encouraging students instead of putting them down. Oh dear.

We continued on as best we could. The class was assigned a final paper on which we worked for weeks. When Christina handed hers in it was nearly illegible. No surprise. I went over it with her and advised her to do a rewrite. When it came back to me it was an entirely different paper. I asked her who had written it. She claimed she had. Why is it entirely different? I wanted to know. "My tutor, a friend of my father, helped me with it last night."

"How much did he 'help' ? I asked.

"Well, he wrote it and I helped with it." She admitted.

"So you did not actually write this paper, right?" I knew this of course. "Tell you what we'll do." I said. "You have a choice. One, you hand this one in as your final and I report that you plagiarized by having someone else write it for you which means you fail and it goes on your record(this was school policy and in her handbook), OR... You take the grade the first one deserves and no one will know about the other." She agreed to the latter.

A year later I had encouraged my friend Laurie to work at ACCC teaching English also. She was assigned the regular for credit English 101. I would be her mentor. One day she came to me frustrated about one of her students. She explained that this girl could not even write a proper sentence and her paragraphs were all over the place/incoherent. What was she to do with this student?

"Her name isn't Christina is it?" I asked.

"Yes, you know her?" Poor Laurie. Someone had passed this young woman through two levels of remedial English and a new teacher with a great deal of integrity did not know how to deal with the situation. As it turned out there were many conferences, father involvement, counselor involvement and Laurie's frustrations but Christiana did not pass that course.

What can be done? There are people who have other gifts than academics. Why do we seem to think everyone should go to college? Get pregnant, start a college fund. NO. Save money in case, yes, but maybe college won't be the answer. Let's be honest with one another and our children. All students don't succeed at the same things or at the same pace or in the same way. College is simply not for everyone. "No student left behind" in many ways is so much doo doo. Some students are "behind", like it or not. That's the way it is. Offer what they need but don't lie to them.

16

HONORS CLASSES

Sometimes even quite brilliant students find frustration in academics. Especially in the honors and AP level classes. The English AP test is pretty difficult unless students have read and written and analyzed a lot. Sections require in depth knowledge of poetry, drama and fiction. The final part requires a well-written essay following a prompt about a novel or play the student knows intimately. How do we prepare for that?

At Eastern Christian my colleague and I team taught a sophomore Humanities course which was part of a four-year honors program to also prepare students for the AP test. We assigned ten books for summer reading (I know, lousy to do). During the course of the year each book and others as well as poetry and plays, all English lit or European, were studied. Students didn't complain very often but one young lady, Missy did. To her parents. Every day.

Her father told me that she cried every night as she was trying to do her homework. She insisted that it was too much and she could not do it. Tears flowed every evening. But, she did do it and went on to her Junior year probably still with red eyes and tear-stained cheeks. We studied the classics from Shakespeare, to Milton to Dostoevsky to Shelley and Hugo and many more. Tomes, some of them. It is amazing what teens can do if challenged. No one failed or even got close.

Here's the irony. I like to think of it as some kind of poetic justice. When Missy got to Calvin College which is known for a pretty rigorous English department, her professors would ask the class if anyone had read, let's say *Crime and Punishment*. Missy raised her hand. Had anyone read *Frankenstein*? Missy raised her hand. *The Power and the Glory*? Again, the hand went up. She loved raising her hand in acknowledgement of all she had read and understood. She bragged to her parents about it and was actually thankful for her tear swept time in Humanities. So nice to hear from a supportive parent. This is not always the case.

At Gladstone High in the Upper Peninsula of Michigan, we had parent teacher conferences after each term. Desks were lined up around the perimeter of the all-purpose room and each teacher sat at a desk with two chairs facing him or her. The distance between us was designed to keep conversations as private as possible. Parents went around to the teachers they especially wanted to confer with about their children.

I was between parents and looking down in my gradebook. Suddenly I heard a rough voice call my name and when I looked up a large fist was thrust before my face. The smell of alcohol accompanied it. "What do you mean by giving my son a 'D'". the voice blew into my face. I caught my composure just in time and quietly replied, "I do not GIVE grades. I record what the students give me." He would have none of it. "Do you know that because of you he can't play football this semester?" It was not about education. It was not about academic success. It was about football. "Sorry. " I said, "But there's nothing I can do about it. He earned the "D" and he'll have to do better next time." The burly Dad left with no further ado. There were too many people in the room for much more to happen, I guess, because that really was the end of that.

Parents interfering in the classroom procedure is another difficult problem. I've had this experience three times. All of them at Eastern Christian. In an AP art class a gentleman, a Doctor, came into my class in the middle of teaching and demanded to see and edit his daughter's portfolio. I advised him that this was not the proper time nor the accepted course to take but he insisted and was apparently backed enough by the administration to have allowed this. I was furious but had to hold it in. My students were in the room working on a project and I could not demand his exodus nor raise my voice nor give him a good kick in the butt which I dearly wanted to do. So I let him proceed with his interference with as much grace as I could muster.

Another incident involved a student paper which had earned a failing grade. The girl's father burst into my English classroom demanding to see and confiscate the offending paper. I informed him that the English Department held onto all papers after students had seen and corrected them so there would be no copying of the same paper by another the following year. This was policy before the computer era. He began to raise his voice and make an ass of himself in front of my students so I gave him the paper. A week or so later his wife (a former classmate of mine) came in with the paper marked up by someone else. She explained that both a person with a Masters and another with a PHD in English had read the paper and deemed it quite perfect. Aha. "The problem lies in the fact that your daughter ignored all my precise instructions and failed to use the documentation required by the department. She failed to write the paper assigned. How would your Masters and PHD people even know what to look for?" I said rather emphatically. She began to cry. Then she told me that her own English teacher in high school had been unfair to her so she saw the same issue here and wanted to spare her daughter the pain she had felt. I hardly knew what to say but we ended by agreeing that the one issue had nothing to to do with the other. The failure grade stood.

Another policy of the department was to collect both the first draft and other drafts. All papers were to come back to us or the resulting grade would be a failure since we had no final record of the paper. One student's paper was totally missing. I had to proceed with the failing grade. Again, an irate father came on the scene. "What's the meaning of this?"

"Your son didn't hand me his final paper." I said.

"He says he did." Was the reply.

"I don't have it.: I said.

"Well then you lost it." He informed me.

"I don't think so." I answered.

"You obviously did because my son does not lie." He retorted. Assuming of course that I did lie. There was no use going round and round. I told him I would do another thorough search and we left it at that. I never found the paper and to this day have no idea what really happened. The boy passed. What else could I do? The father was a prominent minister in the local OPC. I sort of lost a lot of respect for him, sorry to say. I still don't know who actually lost that paper.

Dealing with parents can be difficult but fear of parents is not an option if one wants to teach. Fear no administration, fear no board or a teacher will be intimidated and somewhat paralyzed. Teaching is about the students. No NEA, no principal, no board, no bus driver or custodian or even a building can exist if it weren't for students. It is all about the students. It is not about a pension, a Union, a long Summer break or even a paycheck. It is and must be about the students. Without all the other things a teacher and his/her students would still be able to be involved in education on some level in some way. Think about it. And more, a teacher must have a passion for both subject matter and kids..

17

CELEBRITIES" IN CLASS

Celebrities in one's school are not necessary an asset to teaching but they do add interest.

A bright-eyed, cherry-cheeked sophomore passed me in the hall of Eastern Christian at least five times a day. I never had the boy in class but I saw him often and had no idea who he was. I took note of him because he appeared to belong in middle school instead of high school. At least that was my impression.

One day while I was sitting at my desk supervising a study hall this young man was passing my room with another student when he stuck his head into my room and almost shouted, "So, *that's* Mrs. Fisher?" I have no idea what that meant nor did I know then who this kid was. Later I learned he had been pulled out of school in order to "go on the road". One of my honors students was to go along as the drummer for the group that this boy was with. As it turned out the group was the Jonas Brothers and my encounter was with Kevin. The younger boys were still in Middle School (also Eastern Christian) and this was to be their start-up year. The rest of course is history.

A number of years later my friends Pat and Gordon who lived in Montclair at the time, invited us to go for dessert to a little diner-dive in Lodi. We scrunched into the ancient booth, familiar from our own teen years and looked at the plaque on the wall right next to us. Aha, it was the booth which had been occupied by Tony Soprano and his family on the last airing of the show. We laughed and began discussing other celebrity encounters we had had. When I mentioned the Jonas brothers, the young waitress who was sort of hovering near us literally screamed and ran up to me asking if she might kiss my hand since I had actually encountered one of these young stars.

The fact is there is that idol worship especially in the young but too often in others as well. It is also often instigated with the help due to explicit desire or need of the so-called celebrity him/herself. How silly it all is.

We took one of our many excursions with students to Greece and Turkey. We almost always had the same tour-guide on our trips, a young Pied Piper type from the UK. Rob mesmerized our students with humor and tons of information offered in the most engaging way. We were walking to a destination in Athens with Rob at the head, sauntering in his unique ambulatory style when one of our girls decided to keep pace with him. They were chatting a bit when she finally couldn't take the anonymity any longer and informed Rob, " I'm an actress, you know." He simply looked down at her smiled with that twinkle in his eye and announced, "Right, and I'm the queen of England!"

Nothing more was said about it by either one but on our next trip with Rob he told us he had visited friends in Miami that previous Summer. While lounging with a beer in hand and watching *The Guiding Light* he suddenly sat up, pointed at the TV and yelled, "I know that girl!" It was Joy and she was indeed an actress.

My personal experience with Joy was not so sublime. She was in my American Literature class as a Junior. She was also in my Art class. She was a fine student. However, her mother decided to take her to Hollywood for auditions but still insisted on her finishing the school year with us. The problem was, she was there and we were three thousand miles east. The arrangement was made by our administration that we would cooperate with her tutor in California and help Joy finish her Junior year at Eastern Christian. What did this mean? How were we going to work it out? I got phone calls from this tutor person requiring me to spend a lot of time giving him lesson plans and assignments for Joy to complete. This was not in my job description; I was certainly not happy to comply. I was not getting overtime either.

None of this was Joy's fault of course. I do not understand why parents feel it is fine to push their children into show business. And then to expect others to accommodate their needs/desires. They're all doing well in their field. How well are they doing in life? Don't know. Am not checking the internet either.

18

STUDENTS' EVALUATIONS

Sometimes students will tell you exactly what they think of you. One has to develop a pretty tough skin when dealing with high school or college age students. At Western Michigan Christian one time I got a loud call-out in the middle of class.

I was handing out papers and informing students of the need for re-writes on those papers marked for rewrites. Some had already done three but were still not up to par. As I handed his fourth rewrite paper to Don he took one look at it, stood up and yelled, "I hate you!"

What is a teacher to do with that kind of out-burst? It would have done no one any good to ask him to leave the room or retort with a putting-down comment, which I always have to bite my tongue to avoid. I had to restrain myself more than usual, of course and just smiled, responded quietly and said. "That's fine, Don. Just do the rewrite and get it right this time." That was that.

The seniors in Western Michigan traditionally have "open house" graduation parties which require invitations for the teachers. When I received one from Don I was a little surprised. I went, of course. He approached me and welcomed me to his party but I couldn't resist.

"I thought you hated me. Why am I here?"

"Oh, well I really don't." he answered with a smile and that was the end of that. He had redone his paper and it had been an improvement.

Let me be the first to say I hate grading papers. It is the bane of my life as I've said before but writing requires editing and rewriting so I grit my teeth, "gird up my loins" and attack every pile every evening of the fifty years of teaching.

One student, Jason was so determined to get a good passing grade he asked if he could stay after class and do another rewrite. He had already done far too many but had not succeeded in getting above a C-. Jason worked and worked. After more than eight papers, all heavily inked with my comments and suggestions, he finally managed a B+ and was ecstatic. So was I. If this kid had been in a high school in South Jersey he would have passed without this learning experience. However, I sympathize with all English teachers due to the amount of grading required.

Grading essays has a certain amount of subjectivity to it I admit. I never grade for content unless it is not communicated well or seems to be plagiarized or does not answer to the given assignment, But proper grammar, sentence structure as well as coherence and unity must be addressed. A student's opinion is not in my sphere of judgement nor should it ever be when grading.

I have received other criticisms, especially at Atlantic Cape Community College. I was teaching a course in literature. A young girl sat staring at me with disgust for the first couple of weeks. Finally, I called her to my desk after class and asked her what the problem was. "I don't like you. I don't like the way you talk."

"What do you mean, exactly? I asked.

"You say 'you people' when you address us as a class. I hate that." She said

"OK. What would you like me to say?" I asked. (I wasn't enjoying this conversation in the least).

She just shrugged and said, "Whatever."

"Hmm. Well what else is wrong?" I ventured. She just shrugged again and walked out. I'll never know what that was really all about but I know that I had some how offended her and I felt rotten about it.

Another student in the same class was extremely angry with me for making him rewrite his papers. He came to the front of the room with one of his failed papers and asked what the problem was. I explained that it was all marked and he should fix all the marked areas according to the suggestions I had written. He just looked at me and said, "You're too picky."

My response, "That's what I'm here for." He also walked out a bit disgusted. I know these students had been shuffled through the system and were upset by being confronted with real educational standards. The College does want excellence but it is very difficult to demand it in many cases. However, students' opinions of one should not be taken so personally as to paralyze one's efforts to really teach them.

19

TAKING OVER FOR ANOTHER

When I began subbing for the teacher who needed a maternity leave at Western Michigan Christian, I sat in on her classes for two days prior to her leaving. She showed me some of her strategies one of which was handing out "slacker" passes. She said she gave those out from time to time to offer a kind of grace for omitting to hand in an assignment. Her work load consisted of two senior classes, on AP class and one Freshman English class. The AP's were not offered slacker passes. Thanks for that!

The first rather shy freshman came up to the desk with her little slacker pass in hand after a week of my taking over. :What is this?" I asked.

"It's a slacker pass. I didn't do my homework last night, so I give you this and I'm ok." She quietly responded.

I took it from her and whispered to her that it was no longer valid. "Oh." She said and took her seat. I stood up to face the class and asked anyone with a slacker pass to hand it forward. Reluctance shone on their faces but I did receive most of them. Into the trash they went. "There will be no slackers in this class." I announced. I was sorry it had be like this but I do believe my colleague had been wrong.

This also brings me to the extra-credit issue. Students who have the lowest performance records are most often the ones asking for extra credit in order to get their grades up. This makes no sense to me. When asked,

I usually tell them if they can't do the regular class work how on earth are they going to find the time and inclination to do extra work? "OH yeah." Is the most often response, even though there is some disappointment as well.

As I observed one of the senior classes prior to my taking over, I noted a young man who showed a great deal of disrespect for his teacher. He slouched in his seat, grinned at anything she said, winked at me (I should have smacked him right there, but I wanted the job), chewed gum like a pro but at least restrained himself from spitting. She whispered to me that this kid had been a real problem in her class the entire previous semester. I wondered why she had put up with his behavior but no answer was forthcoming.

On my first day in charge I had begun the class and was addressing them about something (can't remember what exactly) when ten minutes into the class time, this kid saunters in, walks all the way across the front of the room slowly to sit down at the farthest seat from the door. I stared him down for a moment, deciding not to say anything right then. As the lesson commenced he stood up, faced the class and yelled, "Anybody got any gum?" I saw red.

"OUT," I said with considerable emphasis. "Leave this room and never come back. Go right to the office and wait for me there." He believed in my authority for some reason and left the room. After class I went to the office. Jordan was sitting in the guidance office talking with Rev. G....one of our counselors. I came in, told what the problem was and strongly suggested I would not allow him back in class. It was obvious this caused a dilemma, but I was adamant.

After school was over that day Rev. G...came to my room to discuss Jordan. "Couldn't we just try him one more time?" he asked. I said I would not let him back in. It would be either me or him. This was not a happy moment for the guidance counselor. What was he going to do with this kid for an hour each day? Finally, after trying to figure it all out we came to a solution. We decided on a compromise. Rev. G...would watch over Jordan during that class time period if I would give him the assignments and readings. I could do that. So the kid was able to graduate, albeit not at the top of his class.

In Art the following year I noted Jordan's sister on my list. We should NEVER compare brothers and sisters like this but I was a little concerned thinking there might be a problem with respect, considering she and he came from the same home. Not so. This girl was the sweetest, most co-operative student one could want. There's no accounting for personality types coming from one family. Each individual student deserves to be treated as the individual he or she is without any bias which may have been formed due to the behavior of a sibling. We learn so much when we teach.

20

HORROR IN THE CLASSROOM/ ACCIDENTS

Sometimes accidents happen. Even in the classroom. Even to teachers.

I was involved in a team teaching class In Humanities. My colleague, Jack taught the History component and I did English.

One day when he was busy going over some terribly important information about some war I sat back behind my desk to observe the reaction of the students. Every one were rapt in the presentation Jack was offering.

I noticed one young man sitting right in front of me had put both feet on top of his desk and was leaning back in his chair. This looked rather interesting and relaxing to me so I thought I would try the same. I sat back in my leather roll chair which had five legs and rollers, placed my right foot on the desk and was about to lift my left foot also when suddenly the entire chair flipped back on its five wheels and hurled me with a tremendous thud onto the floor. My head hit the concrete wall behind me and I lay sprawled spread-eagle on the floor in front of all my students. I was wearing slacks.

No one laughed. I think I might have been out cold for a second or so. Jack just looked down and didn't seem to know what to do. "Are you all right?" he ventured.

One of the students ran to get the nurse and I kept repeating, "I'm all right. I'm all right". Then I got up and brushed myself off.

The school nurse came tearing into the room to find me standing up but insisted I must come to her room and lie down. She wanted to call an ambulance. I told her she could call whomever she pleased but I was not going anywhere in any ambulance. We did call my husband to come and get me. When he came I walked to the car. I got into the car and went home, lay down for a bit but have never been the worse for that fall, apart from total embarrassment. I was and am foolish. Trauma to the head is serious and could show negative symptoms much later.

I know now how very serious it all could have been considering what happened to Natasha Richardson a few years later. She slipped on ice, hit her head, got up and said she was fine. A short time later she died. I was fine but who could have been sure? Students were kind and no one laughed, then. Later, probably.

The incident did appear in the senior memoir section of the Yearbook however.

Another earlier possible tragedy was averted by a very quick call to nine one one. It occurred in the special ed-or help room. I wasn't a witness to the event; I was witness to the bloody arm and broken window right after the actual accident. One of our senior boys, Bill thought it would be funny (at least that was the version I got) to put is fist through a window. It might have been a dare. Not only did his fist break the window of the door (double glass by the way) but his entire arm went through and cut a part of it to ribbons. Blood spurted every-where. Screams echoed through the halls by girls in the room who were witnesses to the event. An ambulance was called this time. Through much commotion and tons of bloody bandages Bill was rolled out to the waiting vehicle. It all turned out okay but Bill came back to school a few days later with a totally bandaged arm and a smirk one wanted to wipe off his silly immature face.

Girls are silly in their own right but…..Teenage boys (not all) might be some of the stupidest people on the face of the earth. They see no danger, they seem to think they'll live forever no matter what they do and some think everything is basis for laughter. They are invincible, until something happens.

Michelle and the staff of the Eastern Times, our school newspaper, were working on putting the next issue of our paper together. This was before one could do the entire job on the computer so we had a large light table to aid in cutting, pasting and layout, all done by hand. Mark, my colleague and I were just in the hall outside the door discussing a counseling issue when we herd a loud crack and laughter. We ran into the office to find Michelle partially on the floor with legs up through the gaping hole in the glass. Kids were trying to pull her out laughing the entire time. Blood was beginning to appear everywhere. She had apparently decided to sit on the table (not meant for sitting!) and the glass gave way, injuring her in the butt.

She got up and ran to the bathroom a short way up three stairs. I followed her. She was standing by the sink rinsing out her sock which was blood soaked as she was trying to staunch the flow from her seat. "My mother is going to kill me for ruining these clothes." she cried over and over. I saw the blood and had to argue with her to lie down. Steve, our PE person and somewhat knowledgeable about EMT stuff came in to assess the situation.. He called an ambulance. The EMT's hurriedly did what they could to stop the bleeding which was out of control by this time and raced Michelle to Valley Hospital in Ridgewood. I was beside myself, feeling totally responsible for the accident. My husband and I went to the hospital that evening to see how she was. Her parents were there in the waiting room.

They were very unhappy since it appeared a shard of glass the size of a kitchen knife had pierced Michele's left cheek and lodged inside barely missing major organs. The operation to dislodge it took some time but eventually she was ok. We all sighed with relief but she could have (and almost did) died. Whose fault was this? If I had been in the room it would not have happened since sitting on the table was strongly forbidden. Michelle was unwise but she was just a kid and kids do not always think.

Another time (and this was no accident but troubling nonetheless) I walked into the Eastern Times office to find our "editor" sitting there skipping class. He said he did not feel well. I told him to call home. "Nobody is home today, Everybody is working." He replied.

"Perhaps you should go the office for a pass and go home anyway." I suggested. He said he couldn't do that because the house would be locked up. "Don't you have a key?" I asked.

"We just moved and we don't have duplicate keys yet." He responded. This all sounded very fishy to me. I called his home later that day and learned from his mother that his parents were quite concerned about him. He was probably one of the best writers I'd ever encountered in my teaching years and he was certainly the brightest. But his grades were not what they should have been nor was his behavior above suspicion. One of his closest friends was caught by our two administrators one lunch hour doing drugs in the school parking lot. Steve wrote a beautiful editorial about the incident not defending his friend but sympathizing with the situation and much more.

A few years later his parents discovered he was s serious drug addict, had been for years and they did an intervention. The irony here is that I always took my journalism students to Columbia University for a Journalism workshop week each Spring. As I later discovered, he and company used this excursion into New York to purchase drugs. Could I have known? I had very specific assignments for each student and all of them were always done. No, I could not have known unless I had been four or five people all at once. I'm just not that gifted.

About four years later, after much agonizing and research, his parents organized an intervention and sent him to a very prominent rehab facility and he came out clean.

He has been ever since. For many years he has been an English professor at a wonderful university. His wife and colleague, also an English professor are an exceptionally wonderful couple. The boy who was caught is also fine. He teaches music and is doing very well. We thank God for these successes and gifted people.

21

HUMOR IN THE CLASSROOM

Very often students come up with truly hilarious stories or comments that make me laugh, which is a good thing. At Gladstone High each Christmas season rooms were to decorate their doors with an appropriate Christmas theme. Were given large rolls of brown paper to use as a cover and "canvas" for the entire door. There was to be judging and a prize for the most creative and interesting, as well as well-executed door.

I was teaching English. We had done some Shakespeare. When it was time to consider a theme and visual for our door I opened the floor for discussion. Many obvious ideas were offered. Manger scene with odd animals, Santa with lovely sleigh, Charlie Brown Christmas tree done in an unusual way, etc. I had asked students to write down their most creative suggestions, after a discussion, and would read them aloud to the class so we could vote on the one we wanted to do.

I read, and read, until I came to one I couldn't get through aloud because it made me laugh too hard. Eventually, of course I had to control myself and let the class know what it said.

I read, "Have Santa standing a little way away from the reindeer. Who are grinning. Santa is bleeding but it is hard to tell because of his red suit. So, we would need to have drops of blood on his white fur. Rudolph is standing very near him with his antlers on Santa's chest. Santa says "Et Tu Rudolph?"

I don't why but it hit my funny bone. We did do it. We got no prize. The kid who offered it was clever, we all had to admit.

Gladstone had many very talented students which I and Anne, my friend and colleague discovered when we decided to have a school-wide Art festival and talent competition. We had students enter poems, essays, short stories for publication in a fine arts booklet. We had Art work to hang and show in a gallery to be set up in the large foyer. We had a contest for the cover design of the book. One of our major issues was that too much time, effort and support was given to football. One clever art student came up with a bulldog for the cover and we added a rose in its mouth. We called it "The Paper Fullback".

In order to support all this: publication, prizes, judges and equipment we needed a major fund raiser. After putting our heads together, we decided we would do a take-off on the Late Night Show with Johnny Carson. We had this great talented kid named John Kraut in my senior English class. We asked him to emcee the show renaming him Johnny Cabbage. He loved it.

We advertised "The Johnny Cabbage Show" wherever we could. We auditioned acts and had them rehearsed for hours after school. Singers with near professional voices came out of the woodwork. One young man did a whole memorized edition of "Alice's Restaurant". I had two girls in my senior class who knocked my socks off with their ability to sing.

I was having my one senior class do the introduction song and I actually sang trying to get them to sing. I am not a singer but wasn't sure how to get it started any other way. After about two weeks of blundering along I was told that Ruthann was a singer, professionally trained. I could have died with embarrassment knowing how I sounded in comparison and she having sat through it without telling me.

The show went off without a problem. We actually had to do it two more nights in order to accommodate all those who wanted to see it. We charged about five dollars, I think, and made enough to do the entire

Festival. Anne and I did a lot of things like this together. (Our principal called us the "Bobbsey Twins".) I think the students learned a lot from the experiences and it gave a voice to so many talented students who would otherwise perhaps not have been recognized.

22

NAKED AND ASHAMED

I have never started a new class without being nervous. I know that stepping in front of a group of twenty or more students who are testing you from day one is a daunting and "anything can happen" experience. Never in all my fifty plus years have I been able to avoid dire dreams of the first day all through August. It's really interesting that when comparing my dreams with Anne and many other of my women colleagues, there is a striking similarity.

One of my worst dreams goes something like this. I am in the building. I anticipate entering the classroom when suddenly I realize I have not put my clothes on. I never appear naked but close enough. While student begin filing into the room I hover behind my desk with only my head above it. I pray I won't have to stand up. Somehow I am able to wake up before anyone realizes my plight.

Sometimes I dream that the class comes into the room and no one takes a seat. Everyone is yelling or throwing things and I stand in front trying to calm things down with threats. Nothing works, so I just begin by opening my book and teaching the first lesson very loudly. A few people might begin to listen but many look at me like "who are you?" and continue to do whatever they wish. My frustration settles in my stomach which aches even when I wake up.

One of the many things we learn rather quickly in teaching the upper level grades is that you do not begin the year by trying to be a friend. If a teacher comes into the room smiling too much, or telling students they are all going to have such a fun year together, the year is lost. One mantra, a bit tongue in cheek, but also a bit true is "don't smile until Christmas".

I have experienced classes from time to time that insisted on being out of control most of the time. I did what I could to make the lessons as interesting as possible, I tried various strategies for gaining control. I threatened. I did follow-through and that worked a bit. I gave out detentions(I hate that!). I kept an entire class after the bell (never do that!). None of this made a class enjoyable. I literally hated confronting that group each day and I am sure they hated my class. This happened especially in my second year of teaching and I chalk it up to both inexperience and being far too young. I was barely twenty-one when I began teaching high school so my students were a mere five or less years younger. I looked like I was twelve which did not help matters at all. But, no matter. We got through it. If my students learned anything I don't know but I learned a lot and it never happened again. I didn't suddenly look older but I made sure I acted a lot older and dressed as well as did my hair up to appear a bit older. Even these negative experiences could not keep me from the love of teaching. Fifty some years later I still do and continue to do a bit of it.

I am now in my seventies and have just begun teaching some art classes at my local (very upscale) Senior Center called Evergreen in Holland. My students are as old as me or older and all retired. They want to have some really interesting things to do in their retirement so many have signed up for my classes. One would think that after all these years I would have enough confidence to walk into the first class with no nerves at all. Not so.

I know teaching is the specific gift God has given me and it is my calling as well but that does not mean I have no human responses. It is always a serious job no matter who the students are and I feel it intensely all the time.

23

OH, THAT SMELL

Earlier I had mentioned my love of the classroom brought back to me in the smells and sounds of my own grade school (also called "grammar School" rather appropriately) experience. Chalk, books, old wood, radiator steam all gave an alluring ambience totally missing in today's rather sterile rooms. There are myriads of posters, pictures, cubbies and even books in the elementary class rooms today but odors are not as warm or cozy. There are great stark white boards with markers and cloth erasers which smell more pungent and caustic than warm and fuzzy. There is more to see than to smell. Which leaves out a major memory inducer for the student. Too often the visuals are seen on screens rather than in page smelling books. Computers are everywhere and phones are attached to tiny little hands that can barely hold them. But thumbs are ever active. When I was in first grade I still sucked my thumb. Much more comforting use.

And that's just in elementary school. In the upper levels the rooms tend to be stark with little or ornamentation. This is most rue on the college level as I have experienced it. We use computers to enhance our "lectures". We use computers to do group work. We write(if at all) on white boards with foul smelling green, blue or red, sometimes black markers. Technology has advanced to need less and less of actual writing for both the students and the teachers. Grades are automatically recorded into computer programs to which both students and often parents have immediate access. This is a dangerous trend unless we have both students and parents with an abiding sense of respect for the teacher. And there is less and less of that as well. Oh, this tirade of mine. I do hate the over-dependence on technology and refused to use "Blackboard" a program which gives students access to missed assignment, daily grades and who knows what more. I took the course. Got set up to use it but never did. Students were angry with me at times but they got to say it to my face and I found that communication so much more effective.

My fondest memories of steam heat and wet drying clothes etc. made me remember my love for the classroom. Now I love it because of the students that continue to be in the classroom and the lessons I get to teach. Odor not withstanding, it is still a love affair.

I have just agreed to teach a class in acrylic painting at the senior center. Odor is one component of painting. I can hardly wait to get that luscious smell to pervade the studio space allotted to us.

24

NOTES FROM ABOVE

The art room at Eastern Christian is in the basement. It has a concrete floor, cinder block walls and is always cool. It is cool in more ways than one. It has tall wood and metal tables with stools high enough for even the shortest student to use. The work areas are arranged in a U around the room and more tables in the center on which we used to store the large drawings and paintings that other areas could not accommodate.... There are storage closets in the front in which we kept the supplies(many) and some student works. The room also boasted two wheels for ceramics; one a kick wheel the other electric. The kiln was in another area of the school.

The point of all this description is to show how difficult, even with good storage space it is to keep an active art room, having to accommodate about 100 students during the course of a day, in pristine order. There is always green-ware to store, large projects to lay out on flat surfaces and plenty of tools and supplies to have ready for the working projects. So, when people come into the art room the first impression might relay a bit of chaos but as one visitor exclaimed, "Wow this is what an art room should look like!" However, my principal did not see it that way.

He also taught one class of science and kept the room/lab in impeccable order. He could not quite appreciate my mess. Following are the notes we exchanged. (He almost never di face to face. Most communication was in notes dropped in my mailbox each day).

He begins with the title, "Oh my Goodness." Then " This morning Lynda(his secretary) sent me down to block one art class because the substitute arrived late. I just cannot understand how creativity and order can not co-exist in the same space.

I couldn't wait to leave the art room. The substitute couldn't arrive quickly enough!

The things that jump out at me immediately:

> Lack of care for equipment: overhead projector, sink, air compressor for airbrush etc.
> Amount of garbage left on any horizontal surface)do we throw anything out?)
> Piles of ceramic tiles blocking the sink area
> None of the very expensive cabinets are locked and all significantly lack organization.
> While I hold in high praise the creative works that arise from this very cluttered and unorganized space, I will avoid making it a tour stop when introducing new people to the school."
> Signature

All I can say to this is it is too bad that visitors aren't shown a working art room. I am also dismayed that anyone would think we should throw pieces of art into the garbage. Who is he to think something is "garbage"? so I answered.

> "Dear ….
> You are right of course. The art room which accommodates so many students per day and functions as a working studio, does appear to be a disaster (especially to the untrained eye). However, although my first impulse

is to say 'Do I get my early retirement package now?' I do need to address the issue [with] a more serious response. When Phil (the other science teacher) first saw the studio of his son, Bobby at NJIT had the same response: "What a disaster! There was stuff everywhere and nothing seemed to be taken care of. But the work coming out of there is wonderful!" I'm afraid that is the way most good art studios work, the most important thing being the learning and products that are done. So. The air compressor hasn't been used for over ten years. We should place it in storage. We do not throw much of anything out since so much can be used again. The ceramic tiles were delivered a few days ago and are in process as well as in use. We lock cabinets at night but try to keep things open for when subs come in. The disorganization of cabinets is dealt with at the close and beginning of each term and will be taken car as we move to the close of the school year.

People who visit the art room are generally excited by the obvious creativity and work done there. I am truly sorry you found the experience so distasteful."

My signature.

Response from above: "Agnes, Thank you for your response. Ultimately you know that I enjoy all of the creative stuff that EC students produce under your and Stacey's mentoring. Does a possibility exist for 'organized' clutter to be what we strive for?

I am still of the opinion that a student task force in each block could periodically organize the media, conserve the supplies and protect the equipment. And possibly even 'clean' the room(!) on a rotating basis.

The logic presented to students could be, in order to use the space for you personal artistic pleasures you occasionally need to give back something so that others my have the same opportunity without being hindered. I am also of the opinion that if the CRC named saints, Dave J. would be one...if he refused to 'clean' the Art Room I would support him.

My final question- Would it be a good idea to start getting the Art Room ready for summer cleaning?'

Signature and "PS I love the early retirement reference. Just how bad can you be?"

And then, (I couldn't resist it) my ultimate response from a BALDO cartoon: Dad: "Look at this room. It's a disaster! How is this place ever going to be clean?" Response by Baldo; "Easy…Broaden your definition of 'clean."

Another interesting incident occurred at the beginning of the following year. I was again offered a note in my mailbox about a janitor having found "four coffee containers filled with rotten coffee in one of the art room closets. I did not write back. I laughed. Then summoned up the courage to address this face to face. I smiled as I entered his office and showed him his note. " By the way", I said. " The coffee cups in the closet is a sculpture, not real coffee at all but executed so well, it even fooled your janitor, who should have know better, having been in my art class himself some years back." Apologies and comments followed.

All I can say about all this is if you don't understand the process and working environment for art, stay out of the Art Room. Maybe there are some artists who are uptight and anal about their work environments, but I haven'tt found one yet. Even so, I understand my principal's complaints and must agree that I need to have done a lot better in keeping the art room in at least somewhat more organized condition.

I have worked with a variety of principals in all these years. Some were honestly awful but some, Mr. Lucas and Mr. Kim were wonderful, professional men who loved their work and supported their faculty as well as their students.

25

IMMIGRATION SURVIVED BY ALL

When I was barely six years old my parents "plucked" me out my native land, The Netherlands, and transported me and my five brothers to New Jersey, USA. I grew up in New Jersey and still love it albeit the times have changed it dramatically. What was once affordable living is now out of reach or nearly so for the average middle-class family. Those who are there are paying anywhere from 13,000 to 20,000 dollars in taxes for a small house that I lived in for thirty years.

Anyway, we did our first three years or so in small two bedroom, no bath walkup on the other side of the street from Paterson, Hopper Street. We played in the hot, gruesome summer suns 'til sunset while my mother sighed with continual heavy discomfort during those same summers. We went to school two blocks from our apartment down the hill of Halpine Ave. to North Fourth Street. There was not ESL as we now know it but there was a lady, Miss Borduin who occupied a kind of cell in the basement of the school and taught proper English to those in need of such teaching.

Miss Borduin had one wooden arm. She always wore long sleeves that only exposed a wooden hand covered with a white glove. She fascinated us younger children. She also clobbered some of the children with that wooden arm and hand. We would watch her face grow stern, her lips purse tight, her eyes narrow as she took careful aim at the target, a boy who was naughty. She would back up, turn sideways and whirl around with a fury so that that arm would lift from her shoulder and swat the offender right in the head. Bang! The kid never knew what hit him until she said rather slowly, "Let that be a lesson to you." Did Miss Borduin help us with our learning of English? I can't remember. But I do remember not having any difficulty with the language so we all must have learned it rather quickly. I attribute this more to the street and a serious necessity to communicate with neighboring kids than to any formal education. None of my five brothers nor I ever carried an accent into our English speech.

I still believe that experience/hands-on learning, when possible, teaches a much greater and more memorable lesson than all the words thrown at students by any teacher.

Growing up with five boys taught me things most girls might never learn. I can still push my arm up behind my back to zip a dress all the way to my neck because a brother would push my arm up when he wanted to control me. I can fight when I need to and my husband does not care to spar with me even for fun. However, all this living with boys did not make me attractive to other boys. I learned once I had grown up and after college that most guys who might have been interested in me shied away because somehow I presented a front of which they were fearful. One of my brothers told me this, but I never knew why guys shied away until then.

As a teacher, however, this stood me in very good stead. When I walked into a classroom, students generally knew immediately not to mess with me. I'm not sure what they saw but whatever it was, I had little trouble with discipline most of the time. Teaching is difficult enough without having to reprimand, scold, raise one's voice and generally have to exert control. That is not to say I never had any trouble with students. A few incidents related earlier certainly shows that I did.

26

SOME ADDED PERKS

Something one might not consider when thinking about becoming a teacher is the amount of really wonderful colleagues one will encounter. Some of them will become life-long friends (some might even become spouses but that was not my experience). One of the teachers who became a best friend only taught with me for a few years. Her last name is Fish. I remember walking into the faculty room and calling out, "Hey, Fish!" To which she would respond, "Hey, Fisher!" And from there we continued on into a really nice relationship.

Another dear friend and I met the first day of teaching at EC after a grueling morning of introductions, conferences and other awful first day faculty meetings. We sat together on the front lawn sharing a lunch and information about our lives and why and how we came to be there. Kate and I still talk whenever we can even though we now live miles apart. The thing about good friends is that no matter how long a separation is when back together it is as though there never were years in between.

Joyce, a fellow artist and I sat in the faculty room one day talking about our painting lives. We kind of pussy-footed around each other when the possibility of seeing one another's work came up. I was afraid her stuff might be really hokey and she was afraid mine might be the same. What if?? And then, what to say? We need not have worried and became friends forever also living miles apart now. A very special thanks for all the proofing.

On our very first trip to Europe with students, Elaine and her husband Joe were our co-chaperones. We toured Scotland, England and France with about twenty students one of whom was a young man with Asperger's. (not diagnosed at that time). He would be "missing" more often than not having wandered off into some souvenir shop or into an opposing street. We would be yelling his name in all kinds of locations as well as one of us retracing our steps to locate the boy. Why did we take him? His mother encouraged it and we were stupid. However, the entire experience plus many others helped gel our relationship. We have had years of wonderful and daunting times together.

The list could go on. One dear friend just bought one of my little paintings and we had a wonderful chat on the phone recently. The irony is that when I began teaching at EC, Phil actually was scared of me (as he told me later) and would turn down another hallway if he saw me coming. What was that about? It scares me to think I ever gave off such frightening vibes. But we became friends. First impressions should never impose on last impressions.

When I think back not only do I miss the classroom but I also miss these dear people and so many more.

27

EDUCATION'S GOALS

<u>Proverbs 9:10</u> says, "The <u>fear of the LORD</u> is the beginning of wisdom, and knowledge of the Holy One is understanding." And it all belongs to Christ as Abraham Kuyper said in the introductory quote. My goal in teaching has been to help students get understanding and discernment. I believe it worked for some students sometimes. We will never know really how much success we've had and that is probably a good thing. Knowing it all could be either very ego inflating or very deflating. More of the latter I assume. Neither is to the advantage of the teacher. But teaching is a serious thing and ought never to be entered into lightly. As the Bible says:

James 3:1   New International Version

"Not many of you should become teachers, my fellow believers, because you know that we who teach will be judged more strictly." I don't know about anybody else, but this verse has always scared me a bit. I hope that it refers mainly to pastors and such and not so much to me and my kind.

I'm in my seventies now and still teaching but very little. Our Senior Center in Holland Michigan is a fantastic place which offers necessary services and wonderful opportunities of all kinds. The service it is doing for me right now is allowing me to teach some art courses part time which is exactly what I need. I know that my Students, all of whom are retired or semi-retired, need activities to keep them going too. So it's a win-win for us all. I thank the Lord for every minute of it. And for all the years.

ADDENDUM: Readers, please us any or any parts of these 'tools' you like. Just let me know if you do. (ghoshre@yahoo.com)

The Power and the Glory

1. Questions to used for **The Power and the Glory**:

2. Identify each of the following quotes as to either importance to the story or the actual situation and speaker(s).

3. "There is always one moment in childhood when the door opens and lets the future in." (Part I, Chapter 1)

4. 2. "He had tried to escape, but he was like the King of a West African tribe, the slave of his people, who may not even lie down in case the winds should fail." (Part I, Chapter I)

5. "He walked slowly: happiness drained out of him more quickly and completely than out of an unhappy man: an unhappy man is always prepared." (Part I, Chapter 3)

6. "He would eliminate from their childhood everything which had made him miserable, all that was poor, superstitious, and corrupt." (Part I, Chapter 4)

7. "The men and women had the air already of people condemned by authority—authority was never wrong." (Part II, Chapter 1)

8. "Suppose you die. You'll be a martyr, won't you? What kind of a martyr do you think you'll make? It's enough to make people mock." (Part II, Chapter 1)

9. "The knowledge of the world lay in her like the dark explicable spot in an X-ray photograph." (Part II, Chapter 3)

10. "You've killed a lot of people—that's about all. Anybody can do that for a while, and then he is killed too. Just as you are killed. Nothing left except pain." (Part III, Chapter 2)

11. "I don't know a thing about the mercy of God: I don't know how awful the human heart looks to Him." (Part III Chapter 3)

12. "He knew now that at the end there was only one thing that counted—to be a saint." (Part III, Chapter 4)

A Chaucer special Assignment:

CHAUCER AND HIS TIMES

For each of these you are to research the times (M.A.), show how the pilgrim fits that time and present a visual of the same.

Chivalry: Knight

Crusades: Wife of Bath

Cooking: Cook

Fashion: Prioress

Feasts : Monk

Clergy: Friar

Education: Oxford Cleric or student

Manors: Franklin

Church issues: Pardoner and Summoner

Working class: Miller

Manor agents: Reeve

additional option: Cathedrals(Roman and Gothic)

Test on Chaucer:

Name_____10/31/10

Answer each as required: (if false, correct it)

short essay:

1. Discuss the connections between Henry II, Thomas A' Becket and Chaucer.

1. Who is Harry Baily, what does he own in Cheapside/Southwerk and what does he have to do with the rest of the Pilgrims?

3. True/False Chaucer was very qualified to write about his pilgrims because he had been a merchant most of his life.

Brave New World Questions:

1. EXPLAIN WHY UNIVERSAL HAPPINESS IS A PROBLEM NOT SOLVED IN *BRAVE NEW WORLD?*

2. DISCUSS HOW FORDISM WORKS AS A REPLACEMENT OF CHRISTIANITY.

3. DISCUSS THE OPPOSING VIEWS ON CIVILIZATION IN BNW AS DISCUSSED BY MUSTAPHA MOND AND JOHN? WHY ARE BOTH MEN ABLE TO DISCUSS BOTH SIDES?

4. DISCUSS HOW THE RESERVATION WORKS AS A FOIL TO *BNW.*

5. LIST THE MOST IMPORTANT CHARACTERS AND TRACE THEIR ACTS OF IMPORTANCE THROUGH THE NOVEL.

6. DRAW A PLOT LINE EMPHASIZING THE MOST IMPORTANT POINTS IN THE NOVEL.

Some reading suggestions:

Basic Questions a reader should ask:

2. What is the book about as a whole? (theme? How is that theme developed?)
3. What is being said in detail and how? (character, imagery, plot)
4. Does the story ring true? Is it believable?
5. Why does the author think the book is important?

How to make the book your own:

1. Under-lining (major incidents, dialogue, descriptions, forceful statements)
2. Mark important passages by **** in the margins.
3. Number in the margins to indicate sequence importance.
4. Number in the margin where the author makes similar points or repeats something about he plot or character etc.
5. Circle or underline key phrases.
6. Wrtie in the margin or on top of the page any key questions which a passage raises in your mind.

The first stage of Analytical Reading, or Rules for Finding What a Book is About:

1. Classify the book: what is the genre?
2. State what the whole book is about in one or two sentences at most. (utmost brevity)
3. Enumerate the major parts in their order and relation, outline these parts.
4. Define the problem or problems in the book.

Adler, Mortimer. *How to Read a Book.* New York: Simon and Schuster, 1972.

Art tests:

Art 101 Exam

Answer each of the following as required:

6. With what does a line begin? _____ 2 pts
7. Negative space is where in comparison to positive space in a composition? 5 pts

2. What is a vanishing point?   a. a point drawn with invisible ink   b. a point of no return   c. a point on the horizon past which one cannot see   2 pts
3. Name the two kinds of lines: a.   b.   4pts
4. Which of those lines is almost always man-made?   2 pts
5. Define: 15 pts
   a.   composition

   b.   opaque

   c.   transparent

7. What is the difference between symmetrical and asymmetrical? 5pts

8. Draw an example of each. 10 pts

1. Draw a two-point perspective example. 5 pts

1. What is texture? 2 pts

2. Draw an example of hair. 2pts

The 3 following are 2 pts each   (6)

1. Monochrome means: a. one style b. one color c. one shade d. none of these
2. When painting great contrast in light and dark one is working with
   a.   monochrome b. warm colors c. cool colors d. chiaroscuro

1. What two techniques are associated with water color painting? a. dry brush and bleed b. wet paper and dry paper c. dry paper only d. none of these

2pts 15. When you draw / paint contra continuous lines what kind of work do you end up with? a. photographic b. natural c. abstract

12 pts 16. Draw a color wheel in which you name the primaries and each of the secondaries between.

6pts 17. List three warm colors and three cool colors.
3pts

18. List three of the mediums we used:

20 pts 19. Discuss from start to finish how you would produce an acrylic painting one of the above mentioned styles (e.g. one pt. , monochrome, 2 pt, chiaroscuro etc.)

■ ■ ■

What one thing did you learn that you did not know before?

How beneficial was this class for you?

What was your favorite project? Why?

Made in the USA
Middletown, DE
23 August 2017